JOE PIERI was born in Tuscany in 1919 but spent nearly all his life as a café proprietor in Glasgow. He writes for pleasure and is now retired. His previous books include *Tales from the Savoy*, *The Big Men* and *Isle of the Displaced*.

WHEEL OF FORTUNE

ARCHIE MORRISON AND JOE PIERI

mercatpress
www.mercatpress.com

First published in 2004 by Mercat Press Ltd
10 Coates Crescent, Edinburgh EH3 7AL
www.mercatpress.com

© Archie Morrison and Joe Pieri 2004

ISBN 184183 064X

Set in Minion and Bell Gothic at Mercat Press
Printed and bound in Great Britain by
Creative Print and Design Group (CPD)

CONTENTS

FOREWORD
by
ARCHIE MORRISON

Part of my work at Four Hills Nursing Home consists of sitting at the reception desk receiving visitors and monitoring the closed-circuit TV cameras which sweep over the car parks and the surrounding grounds. At times there is little to do, so I have always on hand some book or other borrowed from the public library to read and help the time pass. One day about four years ago a book, *Isle of the Displaced* by Joe Pieri, caught my attention. It was written by an Italian immigrant to Scotland who had been interned during the war and deported as a prisoner to Canada. I found the book interesting, and on returning it to the library took out another book by the same person called *Tales of the Savoy*, a series of short stories centred on some interesting characters who frequented his café in Cowcaddens in the 1950s and '60s. About a year later I came across his book *The Big Men*, made up of stories about the Glasgow police before and after the war, which I also found to be very readable.

In April 2002 a patient was admitted to the Maryhill wing of Four Hills. Her name was Mary Pieri. Although an unusual name, I did not associate it with the Pieri who had written the books I had read. Every day, twice and sometimes three times a day, a small elderly man would visit Mary Pieri in her room and nod to me as he passed the reception desk. One of the auxiliary nurses recognised him as being Joe Pieri, the man who had employed her as a waitress in his Savoy restaurant 30 and more years ago, her very first job after leaving school, and identified him as the man who had written the books I had mentioned. We began engaging in conversation each time he came to reception and soon we began exchanging confidences.

I spoke of my early rough-and-tumble upbringing in Maryhill, of the various dead-end jobs I had taken after leaving school and of my subsequent career as a croupier in gambling casinos in places as far removed as Glasgow and Las Vegas, with the Bahamas and Majorca in between. These stories seemed to be of great interest to him and he questioned me at length about my experiences. Why did I not write a book about these events? he asked. Raised in poor circumstances, self-taught, ambitious, becomes a croupier in the Stakis casinos, works in Las Vegas, in the Bahamas, in Majorca, and now in charge of security at Four Hills Nursing Home. Great material there for a book, he said. Instead of reading other people's stuff to pass the time, you should write your own story. I looked at him for a while, an idea took hold and I replied:

'I wouldn't know how to start. As a croupier I had to be good at mental arithmetic, but I haven't a clue about writing stories. If you think the story of my life might be of interest, why don't you write it for me? You've already had three books published so you must know how to go about it. I can tell you all my stories and you can put them down on paper for me.'

And so we started. Every morning as regularly as the sunrise Joe would appear at my desk with a little tape recorder and ask me question after question about my early life and my progress as a croupier in the Stakis casinos, then on to the Bahamas, Las Vegas and Majorca. As time went by I began to remember long-forgotten events and to live again the days and nights spent behind the baccarat tables and the roulette wheels of the many casinos I had worked in. Half an hour of questions and then Joe would go to sit by his Mary's bedside for the rest of the day, leaving only for a lunchtime break. A few pages each day were produced for me to pass judgement on, and after a few weeks I became as enthusiastic as Joe had always been about our *Wheel of Fortune*.

Archie Morrison
Four Hills, 2004

FOREWORD

by

JOE PIERI

About three years ago my wife Mary began to show disturbing symptoms of mental and physical changes which were finally diagnosed as being the early stages of a Parkinson's-type dementia. Although I realised that her condition was progressive and that eventually she would have to be put permanently into care I was determined to keep her at home as long as possible, and with the help of the local social and health services I managed to do so for a time, even though her condition had deteriorated to the extent that round-the-clock help and supervision had to be provided.

Early one morning I awoke to find her still and motionless in bed beside me. I could not rouse her and phoned for assistance. Within minutes a doctor had arrived and he was of the opinion that she had suffered a stroke during the night. An ambulance rushed her to a ward in Stobhill hospital where she came under the care of Dr Davie, a consultant in geriatric medicine, and from there she was taken to Four Hills, a nursing home for long-term patients not far from the hospital. There she was given her own room in a section of the home, and I could visit her whenever I wished and stay by her bedside for as long as I cared to. The accommodation was of the highest standard, as was the care and attention that Mary was being given. No amount of money could have provided any better medical and personal care than were on hand at Four Hills.

At the entrance to the home there is a hotel-style reception desk where visitors are asked to sign in and most mornings on arrival I was greeted cheerfully by a stocky, powerfully-built man of about 60 or so in charge of the reception area. His name was Archie Morrison. Each morning we exchanged pleasantries, which, as time went by, expanded into longer conversations and an exchange of confidences about our respective families and general background. It was obvious that Archie was a well-read and much-travelled man, and although I am 20 years and more his senior, the circumstances and environment of his boyhood years were not that far removed from my own. There is no great difference, after all, between my own Gorbals and Cowcaddens of the

1930s and '40s and Archie's Maryhill of the 1950s. Moreover, we shared one thing in common. We had both sold VC pies, Archie as a van boy for that firm, and I from the family chip shop, the Savoy, in Renfrew Street. However, unlike Archie, I had always known that the initials VC stood for Vincent Coia, and not for Victoria Cross, as Archie had supposed. 'Tally' blood does confer some advantages!

I had also known his uncle, Elky Clark, the dapper little Scottish flyweight of the early 1930s, both as a customer in the Savoy in those days and as a frequenter of Johnny McMillan's gym in Sauchiehall Street, where I used to spend some time in an effort to keep fit. Some of his punters in the Chevalier were also well known to me. The bookies Laurie Ventre of the Garscube Road and Joe Docherty of Cowcaddens were regulars at the Savoy, as were the Goodman brothers of the West End Misfits, so Archie's stories about their visits to the 'Chev' were all the more interesting. I began to question him at length about his experiences, for his stories were colourful and of great interest and an idea had begun to take shape in my mind.

A few years ago I had begun to dabble in writing as a pastime and I had managed to write three books about my own personal experiences as the son of an Italian immigrant in the Glasgow of 80 and more years ago. I had been lucky enough to find a publisher for them and they had achieved a fair degree of success amongst Scottish readers. Archie himself had read them, although at first he had not associated my name with that of the author of the books. His reminiscences fascinated me. They were packed with incident. Why not have a book written about your experiences? I asked him.

It took a bit of coaxing, for Archie is by nature a modest man, but as the idea took hold he became as enthusiastic as I was about the project.

The paths each of us takes in life, the manner in which they cross the paths of others and the results of such chance meetings are indeed strange. If my Mary had not been brought by her illness to finish her life at Four Hills, Archie and I would never have met and this story would never have seen the light of day. I know that Mary would have taken great pleasure in reading it.

Joe Pieri
Lenzie, 2004

ONE

MARYHILL DAYS

D id you ever try to get a decent job in Glasgow in the late fifties and early sixties? It wasn't easy, I tell you. There was so much unemployment around that any kind of a job was hard to come by, even if you had decent qualifications. For anyone like myself who had left school at 15 without any certificates to prove that he could at least read and write and use the nine-times table there was not much available, and anything you could get was dead-end.

I was born and brought up in Maryhill, together with two brothers and a sister, in Willock Street. Off Vernon Street it was, where it ran into Queen Margaret Drive, although it was all demolished a long time ago. Maybe the tenement our house was in wasn't a slum, when you consider some of the places that folk had to live in then, for it was clean enough, but when I think of the outside toilets that the three families on our landing had to share and the middens in the backyard where the ashes and rubbish were dumped I don't know what else you could call it nowadays. Not to mention that there was no such thing as a bath in the house. Our mother had to wash us every week or so standing up in a tub with a couple of inches of hot water at the bottom of it, after she had combed out the week's accumulation of lice from our heads.

That part of Maryhill was a real tough district. Not as bad as some, like the Gorbals and the Garngad maybe, where a lot of chaps went about with a Mark of Zorro slash on their face, but even as a boy you had to be able to take care of yourself in the streets. There were lots of gangs around; you had the Maryhill Fleet and the Valley Boys and the Norman Conks and gangs like that, but I kept clear of them, and so did my pals. They used knives and all kinds of weapons and went around the local shopkeepers 'at the demand', which meant that they demanded money from them to be left in peace. We didn't want any of that, for it was a sure way of landing up in the clink. These big gangs were split strictly along religious lines: the Norman Conks were Catholic and the

Fleet and the Valley Boys were Protestant, and as it happened I had a foot in both camps. My mother was Catholic and my father was a Protestant, and although I supported the Rangers I liked to see Celtic winning if they were playing any other team.

My pals and I always went about in wee groups so that you were never single-handed if anybody came along looking to give you trouble, but we never went out of our way to bother anyone. Sometimes when you were out in the streets you'd come up against a bunch of fellas who'd stop you and ask, 'Are you a Billy or a Dan or an old tin can?' I don't know what it was about them, maybe they way they spoke or something, but I could almost always tell them apart, and if I didn't want a fight I could answer quite truthfully either way. Either that or run away as fast as I could.

Not that I ever ran away from a fair, straight man-to-man fight, no matter how big the other fella was. I had always been pretty good with my fists and I was able to handle myself with the best of them and more. You sometimes got challenged to a fight and you always had to accept or everybody would sneer at you and call you a cissy or a wee feartie, so you'd go up to the canal banks for either a 'square go', which meant using only your fists, or an 'all in', which meant that there were no holds or blows barred, and I'd get a row from my mother when I went home with a bloody nose or a black eye and maybe my clothes torn.

I remember once at school, I must have been about 14 or so, three chaps round about my own age came up and started messing me about, pushing and shoving and swearing. I put my back up against a corner of the play-ground railings so that they couldn't come at me all at the same time and I took care of them 'all in' with my fists and boots. The news got round about that fight and nobody else in the district bothered me much after that. Maybe I had some of my uncle's genes floating around in me somewhere, since my mother's brother was Elky Clark, the Scottish flyweight boxing champion of the 1920s. He was in and out of our house nearly every day for a cup of tea and one of our mother's scones, and I think I saw more of him than I did of my own father. Uncle Elky used to show me how to square up to somebody and how to fight and duck and weave and feint and block punches, and what the best places were to hit someone. He used to tell me about all the dozens of fights he had, and although he had been beaten a couple of times on points in his early days he had never been knocked out. He kept telling me about his fight with the American Fidel La Barba in New York in 1927. They fought in Madison Square Garden for the vacant World Flyweight championship, and La Barba knocked him down for a count of nine in the first round. Then he had my uncle on the canvas five more times in 12 rounds and beat him on points.

'It was that lucky punch in the first round', Uncle Elky kept saying, 'it was that lucky punch in the first round that knocked me stupid. I could have beat La Barba if it wasn't for that lucky punch and I could have been champion of the world. But even with that he couldn't knock me out.'

I remember my Uncle Elky well, he was a natty dresser and always wore a snap-brim hat, which was very fancy, since everybody else in the neighbourhood wore a bunnet. Only the toffs wore hats and we had no toffs in our part of Maryhill. As a special treat Uncle Elky used to take me to Johnny McMillan's gym in Sauchiehall Sreet. Johnny McMillan was an ex-Scottish lightweight champion who ran a gym above a big billiard room just round from Cambridge Street, and all the local professional boxers of the day trained there. Benny Lynch used to work out in the gym all day and sparred a lot with Sandy McKenzie, the Scottish heavyweight champion. My uncle spoke a lot about Benny Lynch and told me stories of the training sessions they used to have together, and of how quick and strong he was with his punches. Uncle Elky maintained that he was the greatest boxer who ever lived and that if he had managed to stay away from the drink nobody would ever have beaten him.

I went to North Kelvinside school, but as I remember I didn't like it much at all, mainly because there were times I had to go dressed in 'school board' boots and clothes, and the kids who were well-off enough to get togged out in their own clothes teased you about that. In those days there was nothing like the social services we have now for the folk who can't afford to buy things. We had a school board inspector who checked whether you went to your classes regularly and didn't 'plunk it', and who made sure that the kids were warmly dressed in the winter and had shoes on their feet. The boots they gave you if your parents couldn't afford to buy you a pair were clumpy heavy things, and the jackets and trousers were made of some kind of stiff hairy material that felt rough and itchy against your skin. I hated having to wear them.

At school I was quite good at most subjects, but especially so at arithmetic. I was really fast at mental arithmetic and could beat anyone in my class at doing sums. The teacher kept saying that I should stay and go on to further education, but I left school when I was about 15 years of age, simply because I had to find work of some kind to help keep myself at a time when jobs were few and wages low. They were certainly too low for an unskilled casual worker, as my father was, to earn enough to feed and clothe four of a family, let alone putting any of them through school.

Not that I suppose that the thought of an education for any of his family ever crossed my father's mind. Archie his name was, the same as mine. He had the reputation of being a bit of a tearaway and he kept getting in and out of trouble with the police. He liked to break into places and steal things, and never held on to a job for any length of time. Besides, because of his reputation he never could find decent jobs anywhere. He didn't break into houses, but public places like libraries and scout halls and workshops and places like that. People talk about the good old days when you could leave your front door open and nobody broke in. No wonder houses didn't get burgled— nobody had anything worth stealing in those days! Everybody called my father 'Ricey Read', I don't know why, but that's the nickname he went by. Sometimes he just broke into these places for fun, and anything he stole, like scout hats and medals and books and odds and ends, he gave away to the kids in the neighbourhood. Everybody knew him in the district and thought he was a great guy, and so he was to other people, I suppose. He wouldn't hurt anybody, he wasn't really a bad man and he certainly never lifted his hand to me or to my mother. He was good to his family in his own way, I suppose, and bought us things when he had a job and a bob or two in his pocket, which wasn't really that very often.

He first got into serious trouble when he was still in his teens and landed up in the Paisley Kibble, a kind of borstal. He had stolen a rusty old bike that had been left outside a close. He didn't know who it belonged to, but he cleaned it up and gave it a coat of paint, and then did he not try to sell it back to the very man he had stolen it from! He got a month in the Kibble for that. They tell me he got a great reception from everybody in the district when he got out. He kept going back to the Paisley Kibble to visit people he had met there. He got on well with them: he would bring them fags and things, maybe they were nicked, I don't know, but that's the kind of thing he loved doing, nick things and give them away to people. When I think about it, I suppose it was my mother who really brought us up and taught us what was right and what was wrong, and always made sure that we had enough to eat and that we were warmly dressed, even though it meant wearing school board clothes. She must have done a good job, for not one of us ever got into trouble, even later in life.

I remember once when I was about 12 or so, I came back from school one day and found a brand new set of golf clubs lying in the lobby. I didn't know anything about golf, but they looked like a fine set to me. I could hear my father and mother arguing in the kitchen, she was saying something about not wanting stolen stuff in the house, so I picked out two clubs from the bag and ran like blazes down to the backyard and hid them behind the midden. On the way back up to the house I met my father stamping down the stairs with the bag of clubs over his shoulder, his face black as thunder. He obviously hadn't noticed that two clubs were missing. There used to be a nine-hole municipal golf course by the side of the canal, the Ruchill it was called, so I gave one of the clubs to a pal of mine and we started going along to the course to get a bit of practice. We had no balls, but they were easy enough to come by. The first at Ruchill was a short hole: the golfers played their tee shot blind over a hill, and no matter how badly it was hit, their ball always rolled down on to the green. All we had to do was wait till a couple of balls came flying over, then nick them quickly and run off to another part of the course. There we would hit them up and down the fairways and try to copy the way the men swung their clubs. Sometimes we were chased by the park keeper, but we could run a whole lot faster than he could and we were never caught. Now that I look back, those two golf clubs were the only things I ever took that didn't belong to me, if you don't count the golf balls we nicked on the first hole at Ruchill.

When I was still at school I used to make a few shillings at weekends acting as a look-out for the pitch-and-toss games the men played on an open bit of ground behind our tenement. A half crown or two shilling piece was placed on the ground and coins were tossed at them, the one nearest the target picking up all the money. These were rough and rowdy affairs which often ended in a fight and the police were always on hand to break the games up. I used to stand on top of an old air raid shelter next to the ground and I had to warn the players if any police came near. That way all the money could be picked up before they arrived and nobody could be arrested. I could earn a few bob from some of the local bookies doing the same for them, keeping a look-out for the police. There was one bookie at the top of the Garscube Road, Laurie Ventre his name was, who paid you five shillings to be a lookout, which was a lot of money and I always tried to get in with him.

Anyhow, that and the other odd jobs I did for him paid off, because almost right away when I left school he put in a word for me and got me a job as a van boy with a firm called the VC Pie Company, who had a place just off the Garscube Road where they made pies and black puddings and cakes and stuff like that. For years I thought that the initials VC stood for the Victoria Cross war medal, until I found out long after I had left that job that they stood for Vincent Coia, the owner of the place that made them. The job was great, because the van moved around a lot to different districts and made deliveries to shops all over Maryhill and the West End. Some of the shops we delivered to were in very posh areas compared to what I was used to, and I got to see how the well-off people lived. On Saturdays, when Partick Thistle were playing at home, we made deliveries of hundreds of pies to Firhill for sale at half-time on a sale-or-return basis, and that was great because we could get into the back of the stand and watch all the big teams like Celtic and Rangers and Aberdeen play. We could then stay until the game was finished and eat as many pies as we wanted.

As a van boy I didn't earn very much, and by the time I had paid into the house for my keep I didn't have much left for my own pocket, so when I went around in the van I kept my eye open for jobs that would pay a few shillings a week more. After a few months of looking around I found a better-paid job in Ferguson's paint works in Ruchill, and although I was sorry that I couldn't get to Firhill every fortnight, the extra money I was earning made up for it. The paint works were a terrible place to work in. There was a lot of dirt in the place and the constant smell of turpentine and linseed oil in the air made you feel sick at times, but that was made up for by the extra pound a week the job paid. Many of my pals had not been so lucky in finding work and a lot of them began to talk of emigrating. I too was tempted to join the crowds of hopefuls queuing up outside the Australian and Canadian consular offices. These were countries that were growing and were crying out for workers, even unskilled ones, and good wages were guaranteed for anyone willing to work, they said.

My foreman in the paint works was a fella called John McCluskey, a man of about fifty or so, and from him I learned more about the world than I had ever learned at school. He spent all his spare time in the Mitchell Library at Charing Cross, where he read all kind of books about history and politics and things like that, and he keep telling me about the great changes that were taking place in the world, and how we were all wage slaves, and how the capitalist system was doomed and how the workers would one day take over the means of production like they had done in Russia, and we would all be working for ourselves instead of putting more money into the pockets of the wealthy classes who were exploiting the likes of us. I didn't understand half of what he was talking about, so I kept asking questions. He took a liking to me and often took me with him to the Mitchell, where I would sit with him for hours reading books. He showed me how Glasgow was changing and how the heavy industry and shipbuilding works which had given it the name of the second city of the Empire were slowly being knocked out by competition from countries you never expected would have been able to build anything.

He kept on saying how ironic it was (I had to ask him what the word meant) that the damage that Allied bombing had caused to the factories of Europe and Japan had made it possible for these countries to rebuild their industries from scratch, and to set up modern factories using all the latest technologies.

They were now producing all kinds of goods of a design and quality far in advance of the stuff we were putting out from the ancient factories that we had left over from before the war. Lots of these old factories were going out of business, millions were losing their jobs and making it harder for the likes of us to keep the jobs we had. Over and above that, production costs in these countries were much lower than they were here, maybe because the wages were lower, or maybe the Germans and the Japanese were more efficient, who knows, but no matter how often you were told to 'Buy British' in the shops and showrooms, nobody was going to buy British when the same article of even better quality made in Germany or Japan could be had for a fraction of the price. I didn't give it much thought at the time, but I could hear people saying bitterly that Germany and Japan had lost the war but Britain had lost the peace.

I liked to listen to John McCluskey talk about these things and it made me think about things I never had any interest in before. He gave me lots of books to read, by people I had never heard of. Upton Sinclair, an American who wrote all kinds of books about social injustice, was his favourite writer, and he gave me one or two of his books to read. I will always remember one of his called *The Jungle* that I read several times over. It was about the terrible conditions of the workers in some American factories at the turn of the last century, and it made a big impression on me. John McCluskey certainly was a very big influence in my life. He taught me how to look at the world around me and I kept in touch with him long after I had left the paint factory.

A thing that kept me back from emigrating was that ever since I was at school I had been a member of the Sea Cadets and I hated to leave them. I had joined our group, which was called HMS *Benbow,* when I was about 12 or so, and we met in the school hall in Oakfield Avenue. An ex-professional boxer called Tucker McEwe was in charge of our group. I used to think he was great, a professional boxer and all that, but when I think back to his broken nose and cauliflower ears and the jerky way he walked I realise now that he must have taken a lot of beatings in his day. When I think about it, my Uncle Elky used to walk the same way, with short jerky steps. All the punches he took during his career couldn't have done him any good either, although he wrote a sports column for the *Daily Record* for a good number of years long after he had stopped boxing, which meant that his brains were more or less alright, unless somebody else was writing the column for him.

Tucker McEwe used to spend a lot of time watching me box in the ring. I had always been pretty good with my fists; I certainly had to use them a lot as a boy and he encouraged me to keep at it, so when I left school I had kept on with the Sea Cadets and carried on training with them. I was good enough to make it into the Scottish team, and one year we got as far as the amateur boxing semi-finals against England, Ireland and Wales, where we got knocked out of the tournament by Wales. I once got to the finals of the Scottish amateur championships in the featherweight division, and fought Sammy McIlvenny in the St Andrew's Hall, in 1957, I think it was. I got into the finals that year by beating a well-known boxer called Pat Campbell in the semis. I knocked him out in the second round, so I did, which gave me quite a reputation. In the finals Sammy McIlvenny just beat me on points, but I always did think that maybe I should have got the verdict; he had a lot more blood on his face at the end of the match than I had and I'm sure I landed more good punches than he did. I still remember the great thrill I got in the ring when I heard the announcer call out that this bout was for the Scottish Championship and how badly I felt when McIlvenny's hand was lifted up as the winner.

After that I joined I joined the Garrioch Club, a boxing club inside the Garrioch Street School, and our trainer there was a well-known boxer of the day, Big John McCormack, the Cowboy they called him, and he kept telling me that I should turn professional, but my mother was dead against it and talked me out of the idea. She kept saying that if I took up professional boxing I would end up punch-drunk like my Uncle Elky. Thinking back, I'm glad she did. I don't think I would ever have been good enough to make anything out of boxing and I probably would have ended up with my brains scrambled up, like a lot of them did. One thing is certain, if I had taken up boxing professionally my life wouldn't have turned out the way it has.

In the middle of all this, in between visits to the Mitchell Library and in between shifts at the paint factory, I kept on looking for better jobs, and after dozens of visits to the local labour exchange, the 'broo', I landed a reasonably well-paid job that was to lead to very big changes in my life. I was sent to see about a job in the King's Theatre in Bath Street as an apprentice assistant to the electrical technician there, and even though I had told a pack of lies at the labour exchange about my experience in working with electricity, I managed to scrape through the first few weeks of that job. Not that the work I had to do really needed an electrician; all I was supposed to do was move spotlights around and change some colour filters on them when I was told to, and I soon acquired the speed and dexterity needed to keep the lighting changes smooth and flowing.

It was there that I met Rose, a beautiful young girl who worked issuing tickets in the King's box office, and right away we fell in love. We 'winched' for about a year, and did as most courting couples then did in Glasgow, we went to the pictures often. Since I worked in the theatre at night we went to the movies in the afternoon, and cuddled in the back seat of the stalls, or when we really wanted to splash out we paid five shillings for the golden divans in Green's Playhouse, where you could get a really good cuddle without anybody noticing, or had sausage and chips and tea in the La Scala tearoom as we watched the latest picture out of Hollywood. We never went dancing; even though I was pretty nimble on my feet because of the boxing I never did learn to dance. Rose liked the dancing and she was always on at me to go to the Tower Ballroom in Garscube Road or the Dennistoun Palais and even the Plaza at Eglinton Toll, which was supposed to be a very posh place, but although she could get practically anything else out of me I dug my heels in as far as taking her dancing was concerned. On Sundays in summer we sometimes took a sixpenny ticket on the tram, then a walk all the way round in Queen's Park followed by a McCallum (ice cream) in the Bluebird Café, or a bus run to Largs and a fish tea at the Moorings, and all that was really living it up!

After a year or so of going steady we were married and set up home in a tenement on the Maryhill Road. Meeting Rose and marriage changed my ideas and I became ambitious. I wanted to give my wife and any family that might come along an education and some of the good things you could get in life, so again I began the hunt for a better paid job, and finally I found one, as an electrical fitter with the Albion Motor Company in Scotstoun. The company, which had taken over from the old Argyll Motors of the early part of the century, still built motor lorries and vans with a reputation for quality and reliability, and seemed to have weathered the economic blitz which had sunk other such factories. My work at the King's had given me fast and nimble hands which stood me in good stead when it came to sorting out the colour-coded wiring systems of the cars they were turning out. Again, my lack of knowledge of the workings of electricity was no great drawback. All I had to do was match coloured wire to coloured wire as fast as I could, and this I was well able to do, at a wage far in excess of what I had been earning at the King's.

The dream of a permanent job and possible promotion did not last long, however. The company began to lose orders to foreign cars with strange names. The names Volvo, Daf and Toyota began to appear on heavy lorries in the streets of Glasgow, the sales of our vehicles began to fall off, redundancy notices were issued to hundreds of our workers and Albion Motors seemed to be about to suffer the fate of many another British company—extinction. It began to look very much as if I was soon going to be in search of another job.

TWO

THE INTERVIEW

My name had as yet not appeared on the redundancy lists which were being issued regularly, but since I knew that in view of what was happening I was as good as unemployed I began to look around for something to fall back on when the evil day finally did dawn. It was not a question now of just having myself to think about. I had Rose and our newly born son Raymond to look after, and the pressure was on me to find something with as much money as I was now earning, little though it may have been. My heart sank at the thought of beating a track back and forth to the 'broo', with the prospect of having to stand there for hours in a queue of dejected and dispirited men, so my eye kept going back to an advert which had been appearing every other day or so in the *Evening Citizen*:

> WANTED BY A NATIONAL COMPANY Young men of good character and appearance for training as croupiers and dealers in National Casinos. No previous experience necessary. Excellent salary & prospects for suitable applicants. Apply with enclosed photograph to Box 154 Evening Citizen.

I read the advert time and time again and thought hard about it. Without being vain about myself I suppose I was of good appearance, at least my Rose thought so, and I hadn't done too badly with the girls before I met her, so at least my general looks couldn't have been all that bad. I had been lucky and had managed to steer clear of trouble in my teenage years. I never had a run in with the polis, unlike many boys of my age in the neighbourhood, so my character was clean. What was there to lose? I dressed up in my Sunday best with collar and tie, went down to Jerome's in Sauchiehall Street to have my picture taken, and posted it off with my details to the advert's box number.

During the 1950s and early sixties Glasgow had been undergoing another more gentle and socially beneficial revolution, this time of a cultural nature. People were beginning to travel abroad for holidays, the package tour had taken hold, and France and Italy and the Spanish Costas were now as familiar to Scots as Rothesay, Troon and Largs had once been. Glaswegians took note of the way their close European neighbours ate and drank and enjoyed themselves in their leisure time. The strictly functional sawdust-strewn drinking den, reeking of stale alcohol and tobacco smoke with basic toilet facilities which served them as the local pub, looked distinctly basic and dingy when compared to the brighter and cheerier bars they had discovered on the Costa Brava and in the resorts in Majorca, and the local fish and chip shop looked somewhat crude and greasy when the smart snack bars and coffee houses of the holiday resorts were remembered.

To take advantage of and to develop this latent desire for change in the eating and drinking habits of the Scots, a newcomer had appeared on the scene. Reo Stakis had recently arrived from his native Cyprus, laden with delicately embroidered Grecian cloth to be sold from door to door to Glasgow housewives, eager to buy such fine and reasonably priced lacework which could not be found even in the best shops in town. With his acute business sense he immediately realised the untapped market there was in Glasgow for a new and modern type of catering. So Reo Stakis introduced the steakhouse to Glasgow, and in the space of a few years had changed the eating and drinking habits of the Scots. A chain of his well-appointed bars and restaurants soon spread across Glasgow and the name of Stakis was in the process of becoming a household word. His business base now well established, Stakis broadened his horizons. He convinced the city fathers of the benefits that would accrue to Glasgow by the introduction of European-style gambling casinos, and with their permits in hand the NAAFI building at the east end of Sauchiehall Street was acquired by him and converted into a lavish catering and gambling centre the likes of which had never been seen in Glasgow before.

Until the appearance of the Chevalier there had been no legal gambling clubs in Glasgow. There were two smart private nightclubs, the Piccadilly next to Lauder's Bar in Sauchiehall Street and the Locarno club at Charing Cross, both of which had resident dance bands and nightly cabarets, but if any gambling took place there such illegal activities were confined to small clandestine private rooms to which only few could gain access. Many seedy illegal gambling dens such as the notorious Raven club in Renfrew Street and the Rigardo at Anderson Cross which was a combination of a brothel, gambling club and shebeen were tolerated by the police as places where known criminals congregated and where they could easily be picked up if the need arose. However with the advent of the Chevalier gambling came into the open and became respectable and socially acceptable in the city. It became the smart done thing for the middle and professional classes, and anybody else who looked respectable and had money to spend to have a meal and a flutter at the 'Chev'. The roaring business being done there encouraged Stakis on to further expansion. Planning permission for other casinos was readily granted, the authorities having due regard to the increased revenue accruing to the city through the high rates paid for such premises and by the general increase in trading in the areas where these casinos were sited.

The second of the Stakis casinos was the Regency, opposite the bus station in Waterloo Street, and given that more casinos were due to be opened in hotels throughout Scotland, staffing problems presented themselves. These casinos required skilled operators in the form of croupiers and dealers, and while the Chevalier had used imported operators, mainly Greek, French and Portuguese, to man the roulette wheels and gaming tables, the Stakis management decided to train their own local home-bred variety of operator for the new casinos. Hence the advert in the Glasgow papers.

In a matter of days I received an answer and was asked to come to the Chevalier for my interview. I had never seen such luxury at first hand. The thick carpets, the soft velvet curtains, the subdued lighting from crystal chandeliers and the expensive looking furniture which decorated the room where I had been ushered for the interview could have come straight from a Hollywood movie. I sat nervously awaiting questions from the three men who sat across from me at a huge table. They greeted me affably and immediately tried to put me at my ease. Would I like some tea or coffee? Would I care for a cigarette? Had I come far that morning? Then after some general chit-chat more pertinent questions were asked. The first question was the obvious one. Why did I want to be a croupier? I was dead honest with them: because it seemed that soon I would be made redundant and I wanted to find a job with a future that paid well. They seemed to be interested in hearing me talk at length. Now, I certainly do not have a posh Bearsden accent and it was much rougher in those days, but I've never had any great difficulty in expressing what I thought and felt in a coherent manner, and they listened closely to what I had to say. Did I know anything at all about the procedures in a casino? No. Had I ever gambled, even as a pastime? I didn't bother to tell them about the odd pitch and toss in a backyard. Did I know anything about roulette? No. Blackjack ? No. *Chemin de fer*? No. Keno? No. Faro? No. Baccarat? I shook my head.

My heart sank lower at each of my negative answers. I was wasting my time here, I thought, and with a flash of annoyance mentioned that the advert had said that no experience was necessary. Quite so, was the answer; as a matter of fact we prefer to train our people from scratch, that way we can get them to do things our way. The most important thing is keenness and the desire to learn, one of the interviewers remarked. They looked at one another and seemed imperceptibly to nod. Would I come back for a series of tests, including a medical examination, I was asked. My expenses would be paid.

Then I had some some questions of my own. What were the wages? The hours of work ? The sum mentioned left me in a slight daze. I would be earn- ing more in a day than I was at the Albion works in a week, and the daze increased when I heard the mention of the tips I could expect from a winning punter. I don't even remember what kind of hours were mentioned. For that kind of money any hours would have done, eight days a week if necessary. A few days later I was in the McAlpin private hospital off the Great Western Road where I was given the most thorough medical check-up I had ever had, followed by an equally elaborate eye test, and three days after that I was back in the interview room at the Chevalier.

I had come through the medical tests with flying colours, I was told. Fine so far. Two different men were at the interview, which this time consisted of a series of complicated dexterity tests. I had to pick up a pile of betting chips and count them as quickly as I could. Then I had to run my fingers up another pile and say how many I thought were stacked there simply by feel. I had to fit differently shaped pieces of wood into the correct slots on a board. I was shown a series of cards then subjected to a different test and moments later asked to remember them. I had to shuffle a deck of cards without glancing at my fin- gers. I had to execute the same shuffle while carrying on a conversation with one of the examiners. A strobe-type light was spun in front of my eyes and I was asked to name the colours. Then came a mental arithmetic test, the ques- tions to be answered as quickly as I could. What was 35 times 9? 17 times 20? 9 times 17? 8 times 37? 127 minus 61? minus 19? My answers were timed by stop-watch. Thank heavens I had been good at mental arithmetic at school, and although I had been pushed to the limit by the questions I was sure I had answered most of them correctly. After about an hour the tests came to an end, the examiners thanked me for my cooperation, gave me a chit for ex- penses to be cashed at the cashier's desk and said they would be in touch with me as soon as possible.

THREE

TRAINING

The next two weeks were amongst the longest I have ever experienced. Two days after my last interview at the Chevalier I was given a redundancy notice from Albion Motors and had begun to pay daily visits to the Labour Exchange, where the jobs on offer were paying a whole lot less than the one I had just lost. Just as I was beginning seriously to think about a visit to the Australian immigration office, the jackpot unloaded itself through the letterbox in the form of a letter from the Chevalier casino.

I was asked to report in seven days time to the Regency casino in Waterloo Street to begin training as a croupier, although the letter made it plain that this was not a job offer. I would be paid a full wage during the period of instruction, but a contract of employment would depend on my performance during the training period. Now that I had been given the opportunity, however, there was no doubt in my mind but that I would do well at anything they demanded of me. The Regency was the second of the Reo Stakis casinos, and had been open for only a couple of weeks when I presented myself on the appointed day to begin what was to prove the most intensive period of work I had ever undergone. There were four other trainees starting with me, and after a brief introduction to our two teachers, both of them Greek Cypriots and both of whom spoke fluent English, we were introduced to the mysteries of the gaming tables. Before starting the actual training, however, we were informed of one very important rule. All table operators had to be dressed in evening wear with all pockets and apertures sewn up, with no openings or slits of any kind where gambling chips or cash could be spirited away by sleight of hand. If an operator had to leave a table for whatever reason, permission had to be asked and open palms had to be held up for scrutiny by the inspector, for it would be a relatively simple matter for fast and skilful hands to make a couple of high-value chips disappear.

I was to learn afterwards why Greeks had the majority of the positions of trust in the early days of the Stakis organisation. The manager of the Regency was Stakis' brother-in-law and the Chevalier manager was also related to him by marriage. Absolute honesty was of course demanded of all casino employees. Dismissal from a casino for cheating or pilfering in any way meant that no other honest gambling establishment would employ the transgressor, but in the case of compatriot Greeks another factor played an important role in those days. Loss of face back home and the shame of having betrayed the employer who had given them the chance of a better life in another country was a powerful deterrent indeed. The same constraint generally applied among other immigrant groups. Italians also tended to employ persons from the same town or village in positions of trust in their businesses for the same reason, and in the Chinese restaurants now beginning to appear in Glasgow the same practice prevailed. In my years as a croupier in Glasgow I saw several persons dismissed for cheating or attempting to pilfer, but not one was of Greek origin.

Our training began with an introduction to the complexities of the roulette table. The appearance of the table was familiar from the innumerable films I had seen as a teenager, films where the gamblers were invariably beautiful women dripping with jewels, or hard-faced tuxedo-clad gamblers with eyes squinting through clouds of tobacco smoke as they watched intently as the ball spun round the wheel, invariably coming to rest on a losing number, but this was the first roulette table I had seen in reality. There are two types of roulette table, usually of the same size of about 12ft by 5ft. The most common one has the wheel at one end, with the betting layout taking up the rest of the table, but some have the wheel in the middle with betting layouts at either side, and this type is the most favoured in American casinos. The table in use in the Stakis casinos was of the former type, and it was on this that our training began.

The roulette wheel consists of a perfectly balanced, highly-polished, solid wooden disk, slightly convex in shape with metal partitions called frets or separators around its rim, with the compartments between these labelled as 'canoes' by the croupiers. Thirty-six of these compartments are painted alternately black or red, and are numbered at random from 1 to 36. On wheels used in Europe, a 37th compartment, painted green, carries the number 0, and on American wheels there are two extra compartments, one numbered 0 and the other 00. The wheel itself is a precision instrument, balanced on a single ball bearing, and spins in an almost frictionless manner. The ball is usually of ivory, and as the wheel is spun in one direction the ball is thrown onto the wheel in the opposite direction by the croupier. The initial spin of the wheel can be in whichever direction the croupier wishes,

The betting layout is on a green baize surface, and heading the betting design there is a space containing a 0 (European style) or a 00 (American style). Then there are 36 consecutively numbered rectangular spaces, coloured black and red, alternately arranged in three columns of 12 spaces each, beginning with 1 at the top and finishing with 36 at the bottom. Directly below the numbers are three blank spaces, usually located on the players' end of the table and marked 2 to 1. On either side of these, or on one side of the columns, there are rectangular spaces marked 1st 12, 2nd 12 and 3rd 12. Finally there are six more spaces in red or black, and marked even or odd, 1-18 and 19-36. This combination is so designed that the house over a period, given the laws of chance, must win 1 of every 37 bets made on the table, or 2.7% of all bets made on the table. Some American tables with the 00 give the house an advantage of three parts in 39, or 7.7%. The casino in the long run cannot lose, a fact which never seems to have percolated down to the addicted roulette gambler. In the long run the player simply cannot win. A sudden flash of luck may put money in his pocket, but in the final analysis the house will always be in pocket. The 'Bank at Monte Carlo' can never be broken, despite what the song says, as long as the bank has enough reserves to keep going until the laws of chance come into play. There is no skill whatsoever in roulette, as there is in some card games. Roulette is purely a game of blind chance with no ability involved, the odds firmy fixed in favour of the house. After studying the complexities of roulette table betting, Albert Einstein is reported to have remarked that the only way to beat the table was to steal money from it.

The roulette table uses five, six or seven differently coloured betting disks. The colour of the chips, which have a single basic value, identifies the player. Most casinos have differently valued chips which can be used at any of the other gaming tables, and the value of these chips is indicated on them. The betting rules are extremely complicated and have to be understood and applied with lightning speed by the croupier.

The player can place a number of chips in the centre of any numbered rectangle, including the 0 or 00 and should that number come up on the wheel, the house pays 35 to 1. The chips can be placed on a line separating any two numbers, and should any of the numbers on either side of the line come up on the wheel the house pays 17 to 1. Alternatively the chips can be placed on the outside line of the lay-out, sharing the bet on the 3 numbers opposite the chips, and should any of these numbers come up the house pays 11 to 1. If the chips are placed on the intersection of the lines of any four numbers, any of these numbers coming up pays 8 to 1. There are other combinations of placing the chips, which result in a diminution of the odds down to 2 to 1 and evens.

The complexity of the bets that can be placed at a busy table sometimes packed two deep with players can well be imagined. No one man could control and supervise the placing of stakes by as many as 40 players, the calculation and the paying of any winnings and the raking in of losses, so at each wheel there are three casino employees: the inspector, who sits on a raised chair at one end of the table and supervises all aspects of the play, the croupier who controls the placing of bets and the payment of winnings and the movement of the wheel, and the stacker, who rakes in all the losses and restacks them at the edge of the table by the side of the croupier. Over them all is the pit boss, a supervisor who wanders around and observes all the play in progress on the casino floor, both at the roulette tables and at card games, and can change the croupiers and dealers around as he thinks fit.

I soon saw the reason for the variety of tests I had been subjected to at my interviews. There is no time, for example, to count out chips one by one. The croupier's fingers must be trained to riffle up a pile of chips and extract the required amount by feel only, while watching the action on the table. Chips must be seen to have been accurately placed in the centre of a numbered space so that they do not touch a line, or directly on a line or on the outside of a line, or on the intersection of the lines encompassing any four numbers, for all this affects the chances and the odds paid on a win. Later in my career I was to see fights arise and guns pulled out over arguments arising over the exact positioning of a chip on a roulette table. For this reason the table inspector must never take his eyes off the action. He is the final arbiter in any dispute, although he almost never contradicts the croupier's decisions, and if he does, the decision is invariably for reasons of diplomacy. The pressures on the croupiers and inspectors at a busy table are great. Apart from those players using coloured chips belonging to that particular table, any number of players can stand at the table and bet with numbered chips from other gaming tables and can also throw cash on a number, money which must be converted to an appropriate chip by the croupier.

The play begins when the croupier calls upon the players to make their bets (*Faites vos jeux*). This done, the wheel is spun, usually in an anti-clockwise direction, and the ball is launched on the wheel's outer track and in the opposite direction to the spin. To this day, almost twenty-five years since I have spun a wheel or tossed a ball, the thumb and first finger of my right hand have two plainly visible calluses caused by these actions. Players can continue to make bets even when the wheel is in motion, until the croupier calls for no more bets (*Rien ne va plus*). All bets made while the wheel is in motion are placed by the croupier on the circular wooden ledge at the rim of the wheel, and the number chosen by the punter noted. These commands were traditionally in French in European casinos and in some of the superior London betting houses, but now English is used in all casinos outside of mainland Europe. The wheel slows down, the ball drops onto a number and colour, which are called out by the croupier and indicated by him on the table. He first sweeps in all the losing bets with his hands without disturbing the chips on winning positions. He then pays off the winner or winners with the correct amount of chips due to each winning bet. I was to learn later that in European and American casinos long handled rakes are used for this purpose.

It was here that the relevance of the mental arithmetic tests came to me. You had to be able to calculate winnings with lightning speed and pay out the necessary number of chips so that play could be immediately restarted. Concentration had to be one hundred per cent. At the onset of tiredness, which could come after a relatively short time under conditions of extreme pressure, the croupier would catch the eye of the pit boss, raise the palms of his hands and step away from the table, his place to be immediately taken by either the pit boss himself or by another available operator. It was no small wonder that we had been warned about the use of alcohol before starting a shift. Your mind had to be alert and stay crystal-clear while on the job. Your duties had to be carried out precisely to the letter. The wages were too good to risk losing the job by any deviation from the rules or by a sub-standard performance.

The practice of placing bets after the wheel is in motion without the stakes being placed on a numbered square can lead to cheating, but there has to be collusion between the croupier and the player for this to happen. The story is told of a French croupier in the early days of the Stakis casinos who accepted frequent bets from an accomplice amongst the players, also French, while the wheel was spinning, the chosen number being shouted out indistinctly in French, a language which very few if any at the table understood even if clearly spoken, so that no-one at the table knew with any degree of certainty what number had been chosen. The late-placed chips would be declared winners and the winnings paid out. This scam went on intermittently for some time, until the management was alerted and the croupier sacked on the spot. From that day on English only was allowed to be used in the Stakis casinos.

FOUR

THE GAMES

Because of the complexity of play and the many betting permutations possible at roulette, instruction at the roulette table took up most of the time in the early training sessions. The betting procedures were so intricate and difficult to master that at the end of the first week two of the trainees were politely informed that they did not match up to the requirements of the course. The remaining three of us were given formal offers of employment and the daily roulette practice was now accompanied by lessons of dealing at the various card games.

The two most popular card games in most casinos, both here and in the US, are baccarat or *chemin de fer*, as it is sometimes known, and blackjack. Both are played at a gaming table with the dealer standing facing the players, who can be from a single person to six in number. A player may by arrangement take up all the positions at the table. The table can be of any oblong shape, but is usually curved at the players side, with fixed seats for players on the outer arch.

In baccarat, the game is played with four 52-card decks shuffled together by the dealer, which are then placed in a dealing box called a 'shoe'. Usually this is a slightly curved box-like container, which allows the cards to feed down so that they can be dealt out by a flick of the dealer's finger. The players, or punters as they are called by the dealers, play against the house and aim for a count of nine or as close to it as they can get, in a hand of two or three cards. Onlookers at the table can also bet on the players' hands against the house, without being dealt cards of their own. Face cards and tens are counted as zero. All others take their number values. The values of the cards in each hand are added to obtain the full count, but only the last digit is important. Thus if the punter has two cards, one an 8 and the other a 5, adding up to 13, the valid number is 3. A competing hand with a face card (0) and a 6 is superior, because it adds up to 6.

The dealer deals out one card each to the punters then takes one himself. A second card is then dealt out, and each of the punters, if they so wish, can ask for a third card, which must be dealt face up. The punters cannot ask for another card if they have a total of 6 or more, can do as they wish with a 5, but must take a third card if they have a four or less. If the third card gives a total of more than nine, that punter and the ones who have bet on his hand are eliminated from the game. A count of 8 or 9 is called a 'natural' and wins unless the banker has an equal amount in which case he is the winner. In the event of a tie, bets on that game are off. When the dealing is complete cards are turned face up, and the banker is not restricted in the taking of cards if he wishes to beat a better hand.

All that was easy enough to learn—all you needed were a sharp pair of eyes and the ability to count. When we had mastered the rules and the dealing procedures we turned to instructions in blackjack, also known as *vingt et un* or pontoon. In this game, which is possibly the easiest of all the card games to play, again four 52-card decks are used and any number of players can play. Until the late sixties and early seventies, many of the Nevada casinos used a single deck of cards at blackjack, until a legendary player, Stu Ungar (I'll tell you a story about him later), who was possessed of an incredible memory for cards, won $80,000 dollars at Caesar's Palace in Las Vegas playing against the house at blackjack. As he rose from the table he offered to bet $10,000 that he could correctly name the last remaining 18 cards in the shoe. He had no takers, which was just as well for anyone who might have been tempted, for in a show of bravado he named them correctly. He was banned from the card tables at that particular casino, and from then on four decks of cards were used in the blackjack shoe.

The dealer shuffles each pack of cards after which any of the players has the right to cut the individual decks. The cards are shuffled again, then placed in a shoe. The dealer starts off by dealing a card to each player then one to himself. The players place a bet on their card and another is dealt to them. The object of the game is to get as near as possible to a count of 21. Face cards count as ten, all other take their face value. An ace can be made to value one or 11. After the second card is dealt the player can elect to buy other cards, in which case the cards are dealt face down, or he can ask for a free card, in which case it is dealt face up. He then may choose to stand or again ask for another card, or if he has gone over the count of 21 he immediately loses his stake.

The dealer then shows his own cards. In all casinos, standing orders to the dealer are that he must stand on 17. If he has less he can deal himself other cards if he wishes and if he goes over the 21 limit the players win, but the house wins on ties and against those hands that total less than the dealer's. Because the house wins on ties, the odds are always in favour of the dealer. However, in this game, as in baccarat, the player has choices, and to that extent he has control over his game. In roulette the player has no options; he is completely at the mercy of the vagaries of the ball and wheel.

Most casinos have poker tables for the use of the players and these are normally placed in separate private rooms. The house does not take an active part in these games, but usually supplies a dealer. A charge, which can amount to many thousands of pounds per session, is made for the use of the room and table and includes the services of the dealer. The players compete against each other and the stakes can on occasion be very high, with thousands being wagered on the outcome of a single hand. In poker the skill and daring of a player and his ability to bluff an opponent into thinking that he has a better hand than him counts every bit as much as the chance dealing of a particular card.

Poker is played with a standard 52-card deck in which all suits are of equal value, the cards ranking from the ace high, downward through king, queen, jack, and the numbered cards 10 to the deuce. The ace may also be considered the low card to form a sequence of ace through five and can also be declared the high card with a king-queen-jack-10 sequence. Each deal is a separate game in which there is a pot, which consists of the first bet made and all subsequent bets. There are one or more rounds of betting, and the pot is taken either by the player with the best hand or the last man left at the table, even though he may have an inferior hand. A poker hand usually consists of five cards although there can be variations in this number. Players try for combinations of two or more cards of a kind, five-card sequences, or five cards of the same suit. The cards are dealt manually by the dealer, although I never could understand why a shoe is not used in poker, thus eliminating the possibility of a dealer acting in collusion with one of the players or of a card being inadvertently disclosed when dealt by hand.

There are two principal forms of the game, both of which can be played either with five or sevan cards. Closed, also known either as straight or draw poker, in which all five cards are dealt face down; and open or stud poker, in which one or two cards are dealt face down and the rest face up, one at a time in a five-card game, or the last card down in seven-card games. In draw poker, after the first round of betting, each player may draw from one to three cards to improve his hand. Up to six or seven players can sit in at a poker table. The names most commonly used in the US are five- or seven-card stud poker, or five- or seven-card draw poker.

Then you have 'craps', the dice games. There are many forms of dice games, but the most common is the one in use in casinos, where the player usually plays against the house, although games between private individuals are allowed on payment of a percentage to the casino. In this game two dice are used and the game is played on an oblong sunken table. The player calls out the number he hopes will come up and tosses the dice. He must bounce them against the opposite wall of the table. If the dice fall with that number up he wins and is paid by the dealer. If the player calls an eight and rolls that number he is paid 8 to 1, and so on. Onlookers can also bet on the outcome of the throw by placing bets on any of 12 numbered squares on the table, and should the number chosen come up on the dice, the player wins. A 5 will pay 5 to 1, a 7 will pay 7 to 1, and so on. The dice are always provided by the house and are perfectly balanced, with the mathematical advantage in favour of the house of the order of two or three per cent. In private games the players usually bring their own dice, which are invariably subjected to close scrutiny by opponents, but in the casinos the house always supplies them, so as to eliminate the possibility of a player introducing loaded dice. However, if a player has an unusual run of luck, the house dealer will immediately pick up the dice to make sure that loaded substitutes have not been introduced.

As far as the dealer is concerned, in all these games the same rules of dress and behaviour apply. All pockets must be sewn up and the same display of 'clean' hands must be volunteered if the table is left for any reason.

The card and dice gaming tables are also under the supervision of the pit boss, but because of the basic simplicity of these games, compared with the complexity of roulette, the dealer usually does not need help. However, at busy tables or at any table where the betting is very high, an inspector often stands by to supervise the play. The betting is always with chips of varying denominations, but cash, which is immediately converted into chips by the dealer and pushed through a slot in the table to a strongbox below, is sometimes used by players to place a bet.

Hour after hour we practised these games under the eyes of the instructors. We were constantly reminded that accuracy must come before speed. Speed will come in time, we were told, but never speed at the expense of accuracy.

After about a month or so of this we were finally ready for the real thing.

FIVE

THE STAKIS CASINOS

In the building of the first of what was to be a chain of casinos in Scotland and England, Reo Stakis had seen to it that no expense would be spared to make it worthy of his adopted city. The Chevalier was plush and opulent. Thick carpets, velvet curtains, imposing chandeliers, carefully chosen colours and expensive-looking furniture all contributed to the creation of a relaxed ambience reeking of comfort and money. It consisted of a seven-storey structure standing high above the neighbouring buildings in Buchanan Street and Parliamentary Road, for the sixteen-storey skyscraper which in later years was to tower over it just a few yards away had yet to be built on the site of the old Lyric Theatre in Sauchiehall Street. Apart from the building's casino and restaurant, the top floors also served as the headquarters of the Stakis organisation, which by now was expanding rapidly and was well on its way to becoming one of the largest catering companies in the UK, second only to that of the Forte empire in London.

The visitor to the complex entered through the main door on Buchanan Street, then went up two or three steps to the reception area and on the right a curved staircase with an ornate banister led up to the main restaurant. The chef had come from the famous Ferrari restaurant in Sauchiehall Street and the cuisine was of the highest order, not be bettered anywhere in the city. Despite the high cost of dining the place was always well patronised by the general public, even those not prepared to go one flight of stairs further up to try their luck at the gaming tables. The restaurant had a small group playing background music for the diners; that was a big thing in Glasgow then and fairly drew the people in. The outfit was called the Tommy Maxwell Group and was a major attraction because it appeared every day on *The One O'clock Gang*, a popular STV midday programme. There was a talented woman singer and pianist there too, by the name of Peggy O'Keefe. She had a deep, rich voice and had a remarkable repertoire of songs committed to memory; there was not a song requested that Peggy O'Keefe did not know and she became a permanent fixture at the Chevalier for many years. A visit to the Chevalier had now become fashionable, and it was the done thing to mention casually in the office or workplace the day after a night out that a meal had been had at 'the Chev' prior to a visit to the theatre or cinema, and to remark on the quality of the food, the excellence of the service and the great music of Tommy Maxwell and Peggy O'Keefe.

One floor further up was the reception desk for the gambling rooms. On the left-hand side of that area was the casino bank, where those customers fortunate enough to win anything could have their chips exchanged for cash on departure. The gaming rooms also were sumptuously decorated with thick carpets, drapes and chandeliers and equipped with the best that money could buy in the shape of three roulette tables, five card tables and a crap table. These were all well spaced out and the room was large enough to give plenty of elbow-room to punters and spectators even at peak gambling periods. At the side of the gaming room was a small restaurant with a restricted but adequate menu for those who wanted something to eat in between sessions at the gaming tables. No wines or spirits were served in this area. Alcohol-fuelled losers tend to become obstreperous. On the floor above were the changing rooms for the restaurant and casino staff.

It was here that I began my active career as a croupier. The casino manager, the man in charge of the gaming floor, was a hard-faced, taciturn Greek Cypriot who had to be addressed as Mr Stavros. Whether that was his given or christian name I never found out, but that was the form of address given to him by everyone on the floor, and as far as we, the croupiers, were concerned, he was the law. You never questioned or commented on any of his decisions. If he thought that a dealer had to be changed over to another table for no apparent reason, no one ever raised an objection or asked for an explanation. If he were to decide, as he sometimes did, that an operator was not functioning at his best, for whatever reason, he would instruct the inspector to take that man off the floor for a spell. If in his opinion the house was experiencing a bad run of luck at a table the operator would be changed to break the bad run. All his instructions were given down through the pit boss and obeyed to the letter. No sergeant-major in any army had any more authority than the pit boss and I never saw his instructions questioned.

The gaming room was opened for business at 9pm and closed at 4am, with custom building up gradually until at about midnight the tables were crowded with punters, all trying hopefully to increase the stack of chips they had brought to the table. I was assigned as stacker to a senior croupier, Paul, a Londoner with a lifetime of experience in gambling who had been in the Chevalier since its opening. He was a friendly type, a mine of practical information regarding the workings of the casino who guided me expertly through my first nervous days on the gambling floor. No matter how much instruction he has been given I doubt whether any novice croupier has started off without experiencing an attack of nerves during his first few nights at the table. No matter how well you may know the mechanics of the game you are presiding over, and no matter how well you think you have learned all the techniques of dealing in training, the presence of a score or more of players round the table who scrutinise your every move can play havoc with your nerves.

That's why your first job at the roulette table is always that of stacker. The stacker takes no responsibility for the supervision of bets. He is only there to gather in and stack the chips after a round and takes no part in the betting procedures. The gambling chips have to be separated by him into their various colours and values and stacked into piles at the side of the croupier, and this is his sole function. The croupier's task is a very different matter. He is the one who supervises the placing of the chips on the numbered squares. He must see to it that they are properly placed so that there can be no argument about the odds on a split bet in the event of a chip being placed on a line. He is the one who spins the wheel and handles the ball and he is the one who must instantly calculate winnings and pay them over. He himself is under the constant supervision of the inspector who occupies a high seat at one end of the roulette table and who is called upon to adjudicate in the event of a dispute. Paul had the calm and poise that come with years of experience. He taught me how to be oblivious to the crowd of punters around the table and to the presence of the inspector and how to concentrate only on the placement of the chips and the paying out of winnings accurately and quickly.

I found no difficulty at all with the job of stacker; all that was required were sharp eyes and nimble fingers and it was a task that any good shop assistant could have done. After a few weeks of this, during which I became acclimatised to the charged atmosphere of a busy gambling room and to procedures at the table, I was made to take over the croupier's spot at quiet periods and slowly gained in confidence until I was able to handle the table under all circumstances. Try as I could, however, I could never become blasé about the stream of money that passed nightly over the tables. Thousands of pounds, many times more than a man could earn in years of work, were tossed casually onto the gaming tables, and as one who until recently had been working for only a few pounds a week I could not help but wonder where it all came from and how it could be so casually treated. I kept thinking about John McCluskey and his talk about the evils of capitalism and I wondered what he would have said about the money that poured in floods over the gaming tables.

Most of the punters were business types with lots of money in their pockets, probably fiddled from the taxman, pub-owners and the like with plenty of spare cash to throw about. Chinese restaurants were becoming popular in Glasgow then, and the Chev was packed during the night with Chinese waiters unloading the tips they had made waiting on tables a few hours before. These tips must have been very good, for they could lose hundreds of pounds and then come back the next night to try their luck again with more. Some were noisy and objectionable in their behaviour. It was no uncommon thing for some of them to clear their throats and nose noisily and then, in the absence of a spittoon, use any handy potted plant for a spit. One or two had their casino membership card withdrawn, and it would take days for the management to realise that the same persons were back on the premises with borrowed cards, capitalising on the inability of some of the supervisors to tell one Oriental from another.

We had plenty of custom as well from city-centre traders, who visited the restaurant several nights each week for a meal, to be followed by a visit to some theatre or a flutter at the gaming tables. Maurice Goodman, one of the three brothers who owned the West End Misfits, a new and second-hand gents' outfitters in the Queen's Arcade, just along the road in Renfrew Street, was a regular nightly visitor. He wore a cummerbund-type money belt, with £1000 always in it, it was rumoured, and he wandered in and out of the tables, stopping here and there to bet small amounts, mostly at the roulette wheel. He would stay in the place for hours, but his money belt never seemed to change in size. He never won anything, but certainly didn't lose much either.

There was the time his absence from the casino for several consecutive nights was remarked upon. Because of an unfortunate misunderstanding, he had spent a couple of nights in the Northern police cells charged with the reset of an expensive overcoat. A local taxi driver had sold him the coat, which he had discovered in his cab the day before—ownership unknown, he swore. Maurice paid him £20 for the coat, which was worth at least ten times that, and exhibited it without price in the window of the second-hand section of the shop.

In point of fact, the coat belonged to a well-known musician from the Lew Stone orchestra, who, much the worse for drink, had left it in the taxi while being driven from his lodgings to the Central station to catch a London train. The musician, who was very well known in entertainment circles, couldn't remember what he had done with the coat and had shrugged off his loss, until his next visit to Glagow some weeks later, when he was astounded to see the missing coat prominently displayed in the West End Misfits window, which he passed daily on the way to and from his digs and the theatre. He immediately summoned the police and Maurice was hauled in for questioning. After two days he was able to concoct an acceptable story to explain the presence of the missing coat in his window without implicating the taxi driver, for in that neighbourhood nobody ever dared to clype on a neighbour, and reappeared after a further couple of days at his old stance at the Chev, a considerably wiser man. He did however get his twenty quid back from the taxi driver. The musician got his coat back, cleaned and pressed, better-looking than when he had left it in the taxi.

Lots of local bookies came in for an evening meal followed by a visit to the casino. A sort of busman's holiday for them, I suppose, and they came mainly to meet friends and enjoy the ambience. They, of all people, knew that the odds were well stacked against them, and I seldom saw any bookie bet big sums at the tables. Joe Docherty, a bookie with a lucrative pitch in the nearby Cowcaddens, was a regular visitor, accompanied by, of all people, the Laurie Ventre I used to act as lookout for in the old days in Garscube Road, and who had put in a word for me with the VC pie company. I saw him look at me a couple of times, but I don't think he recognised who I was. I must have changed a lot from the snotty-nosed kid he used to give five bob to for looking out for the polis. I suppose I should have spoken to him, but I was still shy about talking to the customers. Besides, I almost didn't recognise him either. Here in the Chevalier he was immaculately dressed in an expensive suit of the best material, with shirt and tie to match, clean-shaven and hair carefully combed back. At his pitch in Garscube Road his appearance was no different from that of his working-class customers. With baggy trousers, rollneck pullover and with a generally unkempt appearance, he managed to convey to the punters the desired impression that he was no better off than any of them. It would never have done to give them the impression by his appearance that he was making a small fortune out of their hard-earned shillings and halfcrowns. As a general rule, street bookies were not given to ostentation; they did not care to have it thought by their punters that they were waxing rich on their losses. The one exception I knew to that rule was the bookie Jimmy McLean from the Charing Cross area, a great friend of Joe Docherty's, who also was a frequent visitor to the Stakis casinos. After the war he had taken to driving round the streets in a white 1914 vintage Rolls Royce landau, always with the top down if the weather permitted. His explanation for this was simple. 'I want my punters to know that I've got plenty and that their money is safe with me. There's no danger of me welshing on a bet!'

Jimmy was an expansive sort, especially after a couple of relaxing drinks, and he spent as much time at the baccarat table telling war stories as he did playing cards, much to the suppressed annoyance of the pit bosses, for his chattering interfered with the flow of money over the table. There was one story which he told over and over again.

During the campaign in Italy he had fought in the prolonged battle for the monastery on Monte Cassino, where the terrain was so hilly and shell pocked that the front-line troops could only be supplied by mules and horses. Hearing that Jimmy had been a bookie before the war, his sergeant reasoned that he must have known all about horses, so he was put in charge of the livestock. After the battle, what remained of men and horses were sent to the huge grounds of the Royal Palace at Caserta for a period of rest and relaxation. There, unwinding after the stress of front-line activity were thousands of soldiers from a dozen Allied nations, glad to have survived the intense battles of the last few months. They ate and drank the local wine and lazed in the sun and played interminable games of cards, betting with the wads of occupation lire issued by Army Command. Every one of them was flush with months of unspent back pay.

What remained of Jimmy's mules and horses had been put out to pasture in neighbouring fields, and he seized on an idea. These soldiers liked to gamble, then why not give them the opportunity to bet on horse races? A rough-and-ready race track was flattened out in a neighbouring field, the horses and mules were graded roughly, races were organised, and Jimmy proceeded to rake in thousands of lire in bets from the enthusiastic soldiers. He had not forgotten his old skills in setting odds. His winnings were considerable, and when, after a few weeks of racing activity he was ordered to report to his unit, he found himself in possession of a duffel bag crammed full of Allied occupation banknotes.

What was he to do with it all? In one of the few parts of Caserta which had not been destroyed by the fighting he had noticed a bank, and there in the manager's office he sat with bundles of lire neatly stacked out on the astonished official's desk. The manager's protestations about the possible illegality of opening up an account for a foreign soldier were quickly dissipated by the gift of a couple of these bundles, and Jimmy left the premises with a bank book containing a balance of some 200,000 lire, which, as nearly as he could calculate, represented about £2000, a princely sum indeed in those days.

The war lasted for one more year, and at the end of it he returned to Caserta to claim his fortune. He had somehow managed to lose his bank book, but he didn't worry much about that. He knew the neighbourhood in Caserta where the bank was and remembered the manager's name, Signor

Scopa. He had forgotten the exact name of the bank, Banco Di something it was, so on his first peacetime leave he made his way back to Caserta to collect his money. The town was not as he had left it, new buildings were going up everywhere, street patterns had been altered and the place bore no resemblance to the ruined town in which he had lodged his money. Through an American interpreter he told his story to an unsympathetic police captain who could offer no help. He knew of no Signor Scopa. He was probably a temporary official sent from some head bank or other in Naples, he said. The Banco di what? How did the British soldier expect to find a bank if he didn't know the name? A dispirited Jimmy was unceremoniously shown the door.

He spent fruitless days making a tour of banks in the district, to be met everywhere with blank stares and shrugging shoulders. Did he not have a bank book? Did he not have any document or receipt? Could he not remember the exact name of the bank? Was he sure that it was in Caserta? The despondent Jimmy was demobbed a few months later and was soon back in Glasgow to regale his friends with the tale of the misplaced fortune, and to pick up the reins of his interrupted career. His 'pitch' became more prosperous than ever, and the memory of his lost lire grew less painful with the passing of the years and the growth of his business. However, he kept telling the story of all the money he had invested in the Caserta area, if he could only remember where.

Another Glasgow bookie I well remember from the Chevalier days was Tony Queen, who ran a legitimate Turf Accountant business from offices in the Charing Cross area. In those days cash betting on horse and dog races was allowed only on race courses, and those street bookies who dealt in ready cash were in breach of the law, as were the members of the public who dealt with them. Outside the race tracks betting was permissible on accredited premises only, and all bets had to be made on a credit basis, with no money changing hands at the time of the bet. This was done usually by phone, and the punters had to be solid citizens with a high credit rating among bookies. As has been said, the majority of the bookies who frequented the casino did not gamble to any great extent, but Tony Queen was the exception to the rule. He was an addicted gambler, betting thousands on the spin of a wheel or the turn of a card. He seemed to have limitless credit at the Chevalier, for all his chips, sometimes to the value of many thousands of pounds, were obtained at the cashier's desk by his signature on a piece of paper. He and Jock Stein, the famous Celtic manager, were always together, although I do not recall that Jock Stein ever bet very much. Their visits to the Chevalier ceased when both were badly injured, Jock Stein almost fatally, in a high-speed car crash on the notorious A74 at Abington while driving home from a race meeting in Manchester.

There was an illegal gambling club, the Raven, just along the road in Renfrew Street which closed at midnight and our doormen were kept busy keeping out the undesirables from it. The excuse given was that they were not properly dressed, but although they always protested they never gave the doormen a hard time, for they knew that the polis would be there at the trot if they did. The Raven was owned by Sam Docherty, black sheep brother of the above Joe Docherty. In the early 1960s Sam had achieved notoriety by suing the Royal Bank of Scotland for £72,000 on the basis of a receipted bank counterfoil which, because of a teller's mistake, showed a deposit of £80,000 instead of the £8,000 actually lodged. Of course Sam lost the case, which had become a *cause celebre* of its day, and was lucky to escape prosecution for fraud. That and other misdemeanours had not endeared him to his brother Joe, who never spoke to him and who would leave the Chev if his brother appeared on the scene. A man was murdered outside the Raven a few months after I had started at the Chev and the police closed the place down. I remember that the doormen at our entrance were doubled for a while to keep out the Raven's old customers.

Because of its situation at the edge of Theatreland, with the Glasgow Empire, the Pavilion Theatre and the Theatre Royal (which had just become the headquarters of the new Scottish TV channel), all within a stone's throw away, and with the King's theatre at Charing Cross not far removed, the Chevalier became a Mecca for many of the artistes appearing at these theatres. Late at night a list of who's who in the entertainment world could have been compiled from the diners in the restaurant. Rikki Fulton and his inseparable Jack Milroy ate there often after their late-night show at the King's, Johnny Beattie and Jimmy Logan with their families were regular customers, as were Lex McLean and Chick Murray, the two famous Glasgow comedians from the Pavilion. The presence of these celebrities would be noted and announced by Tommy Maxwell, and many were the impromptu performances made by some of these artistes on the orchestra podium of the Chevalier restaurant.

We had as regular clients personages from the world of sport. Jimmy Baxter of the Rangers and Jimmy Johnston of Celtic came frequently with some of their lesser-known colleagues. The appearance of these visitors from the world of football and their friends was not always welcome to the management. Some tended to drink to excess; at these times their behaviour left a lot to be desired and a great deal of diplomacy had to be used in handling them.

Some, both from the theatrical and sporting groups, were heavy gamblers and could lose thousands of pounds at the tables. The occasional presence of such celebrities ensured the continuing success of the Chevalier. The first place in Glasgow where you could gamble legitimately, the catering amenities it offered, the possibility of rubbing shoulders with the famous, all this at-tracted the general public in droves, and tables at the restaurant had to be booked days and sometimes weeks in advance.

I stayed for about four years with the Stakis group. I simply state the truth when I say that after about a year at the Chev I was as good as, if not better than, any croupier or dealer on the gaming floor. I was precise and fast in controlling a roulette table. I could calculate and pay out winnings quickly with never a mistake, and seldom was the table inspector called upon to settle an odds dispute. This meant no loss of time between each spin of the wheel, which in turn meant more opportunities for the house to rake in the profits. I was always willing to do overtime and never complained about being over-worked, so I filled in often at other places if the need arose and moved a lot between the Dunblane and Kilmacolm Hydro casinos.

Following on the success of the Chevalier, the Regency casino in Waterloo Street opened soon after and I was asked to work the roulette tables there. The Regency kept its doors open 15 hours in the 24, from one or two in the after-noon until the early hours of the next morning, although not much big gam-bling was done during the day. The players in the afternoon were for the most part bored rich women in search of excitement, with nothing better to do with their time than to come to the casino to flash their jewellery, throw away some cash at the roulette table and maybe be picked up by one of the lounge lizards who invariably hang around all such places. These women weren't big players, twenty or fifty pounds was all they'd bet and lose; the really heavy punters were the men who came in later. These were the ones whose wives perhaps had been playing around in the casino in more ways than one that afternoon, and who could afford to drop thousands of pounds in a night's play and not think much about it. A lot of these regulars came from well-off places like Newton Mearns and Bearsden and Milngavie. We knew that from the taxis they or-dered to go home.

Although the afternoon sessions at the Regency were usually leisurely af-fairs with nothing much happening to break the monotony, I remember one Wednesday afternoon which did not conform to that pattern. That particular day, sometime in the early sixties, I had come away for a short break from the action, if you could classify the £10 and £20-pound bets being made at the roulette table by Newton Mearns housewives as action. For want of something better to do I had gone into the reception area for a blether with the fella behind the desk, and stood there gazing through the heavily-embossed glass swing entry doors. It was a beautiful and warm summer's day, and for that reason the tall figure in the ankle-length raincoat who had just entered the premises stood out like a sore thumb and caught my attention. Normally a doorman would have been on duty even at that early time to attend to any outlandish character who might wander in, but for whatever reason that Wednesday afternoon there was no one on duty at the Regency door.

The raincoat-clad figure stood for a moment, and instead of coming up to the reception desk as would have been normal, turned off sharply towards the toilet area. My curiosity aroused, I followed him in and stood at a urinal a few feet away. I took one sideways glance at him and made a hurried exit. A quick dash to the phone and I dialled 999. 'Police! There's a man in here with a shotgun under his coat. Come quick!'

I put the phone down and waited. A minute passed, the man emerged from the toilets, looked around and proceeded to climb slowly up the broad stairs leading up to the administration area where Stakis had his private office. He was not even halfway up when a police car screeched to a halt in the street outside. The suspect quickly identified, he was buried under an avalanche of blue-clad bodies and stripped of his raincoat to reveal a wicked-looking double-barrelled shotgun. He was marched off to the police station and questioned. Mr Lukas had been the owner of the Rainbow Café, an establishment situated next to the newly opened Regency casino. A year or so after the opening of the Regency, the lease of the adjoining Rainbow Café came to an end, and the premises were acquired by Reo Stakis for use as an amusement arcade and one-arm bandit emporium. It was the policy of the Stakis organisation to keep their casinos free from gaming machines. These lowered the tone of a place, it was felt, but since these places were so profitable Stakis had no objection whatsoever to setting up amusement arcades as a separate entity as close to the main casino as possible, and jumped at the chance of acquiring the lease of the adjoining Rainbow Café. It did not cross his mind, or perhaps it did, that Mr Lukas stood to lose a lucrative site without a pennyworth of compensation, but Lukas, left out in the cold, brooded deep and long about the injustice done to him. Hence the shotgun. He had intended to point the thing at Stakis and frighten the daylights out of him.

Lest he be tempted to pull the trigger, he had not brought any cartridges with him, and the gun was not loaded. The newspapers of the day made much of the affair, and Lukas, charged with the possession of an offensive weapon, was let off with a stern admonishment by the presiding magistrate.

The Regency was the first casino in Glasgow to employ women dealers, although I was told that many flashy European houses employed good-looking female dealers in considerable numbers to give the gambling rooms a touch of glamour. Our two women, who had come up from one of the big

London casinos, were certainly smashing-looking birds and knew the game inside out. They worked the card tables mainly, although they were allowed to take over at the roulette wheel during quiet periods. They wore their low-cut dresses in a way which exuded the maximum of sexy glamour, thus encouraging the male punters to act out the big gambler role at their table.

First-class croupiers and dealers are not easy to come by, and the best are at a premium. In the same way that football clubs have scouts touring around the world looking for good players, the casinos of this world follow the same procedure in an attempt to recruit the best in croupiers and dealers. One night at the Regency I was working the roulette table during a very busy period, when two players came in and bought and lost a few quid's worth of chips over a couple of hours play. They did the same thing for four consecutive nights, going from table to table during the course of their stay. The inspector on the floor with me, who also acted as my relief during rest periods was a London Italian by the name of Mario, and as the two punters were leaving after their last visit they asked if they could speak to us privately somewhere the next day. Over a coffee at a nearby café the next morning they introduced themselves as scouts for a group of casinos in the Bahamas, and offered the two of us a contract to work in a casino in Nassau. The offer was for an 18-month contract with free accommodation at a third more than the wages we were getting in Glasgow. When I tell you that we were earning about £280 a week plus about eighty quid or so a week in tips with Stakis, at a time when the average wage was probably about £40 a week or so, you can imagine the attraction of the money that was on offer. Plus the fact that it was all going to be tax free made it an offer that nobody could refuse. Mario did not hesitate for a second and accepted right away, but he was a single man and had nobody else to consider. I was keen to accept too, but Rose had to be consulted and her approval obtained, so I told the scouts I would let them know no later than the next day.

It was just a few months after this that a no-tipping rule was imposed in all of the Stakis casinos. The tips given to any of the staff, in the casino or in the restaurant, were all pooled. One half of these tips was kept back by the management and the other half was distributed evenly among the workers, including those who had no contact with customers, which was fair enough, since the back-room staff contributed as much as anyone else to ultimate customer satisfaction. The distribution was made monthly as an unspecified extra in the paypacket, as part of the wages and with tax deducted. Hearsay had it that higher up in the management the tips were shared in cash and on a weekly basis. Complaints were made, as a result of which, after much accusation and counter-accusation, a no-tipping rule was established in all of the Stakis establishments, which meant a considerable loss to all concerned and gave rise to dark mutterings against those who had brought the matter up. Half a loaf is better than none, even if there are some who are keeping the bulk of the bread for themselves.

SIX

THE NASSAU GRAND

After the meeting with the two scouts I couldn't get home fast enough to consult Rose. I filled her in about the offer the scouts had made me, and the money they had offered for the job in the Bahamas. By this time we had had an addition to the family; our second son Craig had appeared on the scene, so at first Rose didn't at all relish the idea of being left alone at home with two weans to look after. I didn't like that part of it either, being separated from Rose and from the kids, but it was obvious that the extra money would mean that we could build a foundation for a secure future for us all, so it didn't take very long for Rose to agree to the move, although somewhat apprehensively. It was only going to be for eighteen months, after all, and it wouldn't be a continuous absence for I had been promised three holiday breaks in that period. So the next day I handed in my three weeks' notice to the Chevalier. A week after that Rose bid me a tearful farewell at Glasgow airport and a few hours later I was sitting comfortably and eagerly on a British Airways flight from Heathrow to Nassau.

My debut at the Chevalier four years previously had been a bit of a culture shock. To someone brought up in the deprived area that was the Maryhill of my boyhood, the luxury of the Chev and the manner in which the customers there flashed their money around had seemed unreal. The very same feeling came back at to me at the first sight of the Bahamas and the Nassau Grand Hotel that was to be my place of work. The white sandy beaches, the palm trees waving in a warm and gentle sea breeze, the brilliant blue sky dotted with fluffy white clouds were like something out of a travel brochure, and since I had left a dreich and dismal Glasgow on a cold wet day in late winter, a bigger contrast could not have been imagined. Situated on the edge of the beach, the Nassau Grand was a long white structure of about 500 rooms with the casino in the centre. The gaming rooms were huge: there were twelve roulette tables, six card tables, three crap tables, and positioned in a vast hall at the entrance there were row upon row of gaming machines, one-armed bandits or fruit machines as we called them back home—well over a hundred of them. None of the casinos I had worked in Scotland had machines of that sort; the only ones I had ever seen had been in amusement arcades and cafes and I had never imagined there could have been so many of them together in the one place. There were score upon score of players clustered around them, feeding dollar after dollar into the cash slots and pulling madly at the levers, barely giving time for the losing symbols to come to a stop. There was music playing in the background, but this was drowned out by the incessant whirring and clicking of gears and levers, interspersed from time to time by the clatter of dollars tumbling down as a winning combination came up. I was later to find out that the gaming machines could be adjusted to give the house any odds the management cared to fix. In the Nassau Grand they were set to give the house a 9% advantage, and the odds against a jackpot were usually set at about 500 to one or so.

On the night before I was due to start work at the tables I caused quite a scene to be played out at the one-armed bandits. An American cruise ship had just arrived for a three-day stop at the hotel, and a group of passengers were busily engaged in pumping dollars as fast as they could into the machines. I stood and watched one fella, a beefy guy, slightly the worse for drink, with a cowboy hat full of dollars under his arm, feeding one dollar after another into a machine without any success, winning something now and then but feeding it all back, and soon coming to the end of his stock of dollars. His money finished, he aimed an angry kick at the machine and stood back unsteadily to light a cigar. The machine stood vacant for a few minutes, then a woman came along, put in a couple of dollars, lost them and walked away. I took her place at the machine, took a dollar from my pocket, fed it into the slot, pulled the handle and watched in disbelief as three bars came up and a flood of jackpot dollars poured down. The American gave a bellow of rage, threw his hat on the floor, let out a stream of curses and proceeded to vent his rage with a series of kicks at the offending machine, He was immediately pounced on by the ever-present bouncers, and after a slight scuffle was dumped on the pavement outside. Without doing a stroke of work at the casino I was immediately about $100 the richer! It was only the next day, when I was briefed by my pit boss about the rules and regulations of the house, that I learned that casino employees could not participate in any form of gambling on the premises. Hearing that, I owned up to my sin on the previous evening. He laughed; as far as he was concerned my employment had started only that very minute.

There were two restaurants and half a dozen or so bars in the complex, all differently decorated and with their own special ambience. Next to them was the entertainment and dance area, a shallowly-tiered room with a small stage and dance floor at the centre. Row after row of tables were spaced out on the tiers, and here the customer could order up all kinds of exotic Caribbean drinks while watching the cabaret show put on every evening. Compared to the opulence and size and the goings on at the Nassau Grand, the Glasgow casinos now seemed to me drab and lifeless. I quickly got used to my new environment. A roulette table and a card game or a craps session are the same the world over, and punters everywhere are more or less the same too, maybe not in their dress and accents, but certainly in their behaviour. The ones in the Bahamas were flashier in their dress than the ones I had become accustomed to in Scotland and very different in their accents. Many of them were tourists from the US and they positively reeked of cash, the men with their Rolex wristwatches and the women dripping with expensive-looking jewels. At weekends the hotel's 500 or so rooms were filled to overflowing by arrivals from Florida and sometimes from New York come for a weekend's sun, booze, broads and baccarat.

A touch of colour was added in a literal sense by the ethnic background of some of these tourists. There was still a colour bar in the US casinos, and a good number of the flights arriving at Nassau airport were full of African Americans unable to frequent the casinos in their own land. They, if anything, were even more flamboyant in dress and behaviour than their white compatriots and seemed to have every bit as much money to burn. They all had one thing in common, a pathological desire to get rid of their wealth as quickly as possible. Had I thought the Chev customers were well off? Well, the punters at the Grand Nassau made them seem paupers by comparison. Where I had been used to bets of twenty, fifty, even a hundred pounds, here the bets were in hundreds, in thousands and in multiples of thousands.

The gaming rooms were open for about 20 hours every day and busy most of the time, with the dealers having to work all kinds of weird shifts to man the tables. Unlike the Stakis casinos, where a croupier at busy periods was ordered to take a rest every two hours or so to maintain efficiency, the Grand Nassau let you work at a stance for twice as long, or as long as the pit boss considered that you were still functioning adequately. There were times when, coming off a shift, I would stretch out on the beach for a laze in the sun, ready for an afternoon's rest, only to hear my name called out on the tannoy and find that I was being asked to stand in for the absence of some dealer or other.

I began to take an interest in the history of the Bahamas and in how the present gambling set-up had developed, but since there was nothing in Nassau even remotely resembling the Mitchell Library, for sources I had to make do with the *Nassau Guardian*, a Bahamaian newspaper, and from their archives I was able to piece together some interesting facts. Until the late fifties gambling had been illegal there, but had been tolerated in some clubs in the winter months for the benefit of the wealthy visitors from the cruise ships. At the time the political scene in the Bahamas was dominated by a political group known as the Bay Street Boys, a white political élite based on Bay St., the main commercial street in Nassau. Their leader was Stafford Sands, who became known as the father of Bahamian tourism and was later given a knighthood. Stafford Sands had a more than nodding acquaintance with Myer Lansky, the associate of the American mobsters Lucky Luciano and Frank Costello, all of whom had large hotel and gambling interests in Havana. Then Castro came to power in Cuba, the corrupt president Batista fled to Florida with his Mafia backing, and the American mobsters began looking around for other outlets for the torrents of crime money produced by their rackets in the US and for somewhere to rebuild their Cuban gambling rackets.

The Mafia had extensive connections in the Bahamas dating back to Prohibition days, when the islands were used as a base for the smuggling of bootleg liquor into the USA. In those days shiploads of liquor would be quite legally imported into the Bahamas, from there to be smuggled into the US along the thousands of miles of unguarded Florida and Gulf of Mexico coastline. Some of the bootleg booze was delivered almost directly to the consumers in the Detroit area. Thousands of barrels of bulk whisky would be transferred from the big merchant ships onto smaller boats which sailed north into the St Lawrence river, then up into Lake Ontario. There the liquor was delivered to a distillery in the Canadian town of Windsor, where a pipeline had been laid under the waters of the Detroit River to a clandestine bottling plant on the American side. The whisky was pumped through across the river, bottled with fake labels and sold at enormous profit. This procedure could be carried out only in the summer months, for in winter the St Lawrence froze solid for four months and was closed to all navigation

Since the repeal of Prohibition Lansky had been a frequent visitor to Nassau, and with the downfall of the Havana casinos and the huge loss of revenue to his crime syndicate he reasoned that gambling in the Bahamas could be just as profitable to them as the Cuban connection had been, so he approached Stafford Sands to discuss the possibility of setting up a chain of hotels and casinos where he, Lansky, would have the gambling rights, a concession for which he was prepared to pay handsomely. Lansky's proposals must have been satisfactory, for Sands used his political connections and had the existing law modified to allow 'certificates of exemption' to be issued for special cases in respect of the anti-gambling laws, and luxurious hotels with casinos attached began to sprout up throughout the islands. Overall responsibility for these developments was in the hands of Wallace Groves, a Wall Street promoter who had recently served a prison sentence in the USA for defrauding through the mail and was now living in style in the Bahamas. Companies were set up to finance new resorts, and certificates of exemption were issued by the score.

The companies responsible for all this building activity were mainly registered in the Cayman Islands, and their register of directors included the names of spouses and relatives of prominent Mafia families. Alarmed by newspaper reports of possible criminal activities in the islands, a Royal Commission of Enquiry was set up in 1967 to investigate the role of organised crime in the development of gambling in the Bahamas, and it noted: 'At one stage we began to wonder if the name "Myer Lansky" was applied to more than one person, so all-pervasive was it in the investigations we were carrying out.'

But the new gambling set-up in the Bahamas was in no way comparable to the corrupt and criminal activities that had been the norm in Cuba. There, the casinos existed for the private profit of the few criminals who controlled them, whereas in the Bahamas they represented the hope of Stafford Sand's political party to bring development and prosperity to the nation; if in the process some shady deals had to be made with shady characters, then so be it. In the same year an investigative journalist in the *Wall Street Journal* wrote a series of articles listing the large sums paid out to Bahamaian officials as consultancy fees by development companies and questioned the honesty of these payments. Sir Stafford Sands was deeply implicated and the ensuing scandal brought down Sands and the Bay Street Boys.

The new government under Lynden Pindling, an ethnic Bahamanian, realised that to achieve the goals of social progress hoped for by his government, money was needed for the roads, water, sewage and electricity basic to a modern state's needs, and that the major source of money was the taxation levied on the hotels and legal gambling. He organised the setting up of an organisation under government supervision to be known as Intertel to get rid of the Mafia criminals behind the casinos, and after a short time gambling in the Bahamas became respectable. The seal on this respectability came with the arrival of the multi-millionaire American Howard Hughes, who bought out the Paradise Island resort with its complex of hotels and beaches and set up his headquarters there. Hughes also contributed to the funding of Intertel, and so impressed was he by the manner in which it went about rooting out the criminal elements in gambling that he turned over to it all security arrangements for his expanding casino ventures in Las Vegas. Hughes had moved into

Las Vegas in 1967 when he bought the newly-built Desert Inn from a mysterious Cleveland group, and had expanded his operations to become the largest casino owner in Nevada. Because of the fame given to it by Hughes' involvement, Intertel was to become the largest security agency in the US.

All this reading in the newspaper archives helped to explain a lot of things. A good percentage of the staff at the Nassau Grand, in the gaming rooms as in the main hotel, were Spanish-speaking, and although their English was good enough to get on with their jobs they all spoke Spanish amongst themselves. They were Cuban, both white and coloured, and had followed the exodus of the casinos to their new incarnatioon in the Bahamas. Practically all of the American tourists were ex-Cuba clients who had simply followed the gambling to its new spot in the Caribbean. Cuba or Nassau, it didn't matter to them; they just got on a boat or plane in Florida or New York, and at the end of the journey, which took just about the same time, they found themselves in the same environment as in Cuba: plenty of sun, sumptuous hotels, lavishly appointed casinos and cheap booze and sex to saturation point for those who sought it.

It was not just the run-of-the mill tourists who took the new trail to Nassau; the wealthy and the famous followed too. George Raft, a little stiffer and greyer than he had been in his tango dancer and film star days, could occasionally be seen sauntering elegantly through the gaming rooms. Rumour had it that he had lost millions in the Cuba debacle, and he now was trying to recoup some of his losses by using his past mobster connections to gain a foothold in this new gambling paradise. The Hollywood smart set also changed their destination. Instead of Havana, Nassau became their port of call for gambling and *la dolce vita*. Budding film stars and starlets came in droves. Members of the legendary Sinatra Rat Pack from Hollywood and Las Vegas were a common sight in the Bahamas casinos.

Sinatra himself was a frequent visitor, often accompanied by Sammy Davis Jr, who must have revelled in the fact that here he could mix freely with the guests in the casinos, bars and restaurants, regardless of his colour, something he could never have done in the casinos of the US in those years. There was irony in the fact that although he was a much sought-after entertainer in the Las Vegas casinos, his colour saw to it that he had to enter and leave the premises by the back door, and could not join the other guests in the body of the hotel. Davis was a heavy punter at the tables and could occasionally lose considerable sums of money. I myself raked in the best part of $10,000 from him at the roulette table in the Nassau Grand at one session. He always handled his own money, whereas Sinatra, who was known to be a heavy gambler, was never seen to place a bet on the roulette table or to turn a card at baccarat himself. The chips were handled by one of his numerous bodyguards, all of them large and formidable types who saw to it that no tourist, turned hysterical at the sight of the famous star, could pester him with demands for autographs, or attempt to smother him with kisses, as was often the case when he was spotted by the giggling over-sexed, over-weight and over-painted women always to be found in the gaming rooms.

The lack of a colour bar in the new luxurious Bahamas hotels and casinos resulted in an influx of coloured holidaymakers and gambling enthusiasts from the US, and the guest list at the Nassau Grand sometimes read like the Who's Who of black entertainers, with names like Cab Calloway, Benny Carter and Ella Fitzgerald frequently appearing on it. Aside from Sammy Davis Jr, the only other black entertainer I saw who bet anything much at the tables was Cab Calloway. He was addicted to the crap tables, and loved to shoot craps for hours on end against the house.

The funny thing was, although all the members of the famous Sinatra Rat Pack were frequent visitors to the Bahamas casinos, only Sinatra and Sammy Davis were easily recognisable. Peter Lawford and Joey Bishop could wander at will through the rooms without drawing a second glance, although until it was explained to me I had no idea who Joey Bishop was. One night I dealt cards at the baccarat table for a full hour to a vaguely familiar figure in dark glasses, to be told after his departure with about two or three hundred dollars or so of winnings, that I had been dealing to Dean Martin, who was subsequently to become a regular visitor to my baccarat table at the Sands in Las Vegas. I was to learn from later experiences in Vegas that most film stars preferred to go about their leisure activities unrecognised by the public who had made them famous. A pair of glasses, a slight change of hair style and make-up suffices to completely change an appearance.

It was at the Nassau Grand baccarat tables that I was to have my first experience of what really big gambling could be like. At the Chevalier in Glasgow £100 bets were a big thing to me, and when that grew to the £1000 bets I was becoming accustomed to in the Nassau Grand I thought that the absolute peak of gambling fever had been reached. I had heard tales of huge losses and wins of course, but I shrugged these off as being just tall tales, until one day I was to experience personally the size of the bets a really big-time gambler can make.

One morning I was called to the manager's office to be informed that a call had just come in booking a complete baccarat table for the exclusive use of one party that night, and that I was to be the dealer at the game. The table had been booked in the name of a Kerry Packer. The name then didn't mean anything to me, but one of the old Cuba hands explained that Packer was a young Australian who used to bet heavily in the Havana casinos and that his family were the owners of radio and TV stations in Australia. The same old-timer also mentioned that the management must have had a lot of confidence in me to put me in charge of a privately booked table, because a private table usually meant that the betting was going to be heavy.

Rules can vary in small detail from casino to casino, but the basics for baccarat are the same everywhere. At the Nassau Grand the game was played at a six-player table, with four decks of cards put together and shuffled and then dealt from a shoe. The house dealer must adhere to the policy of his casino, which usually is not to draw another card on a total which adds up to six, and this was the policy at the Nassau Grand. The laws of chance dictate that over a protracted period of play, not going above such a number will always give the house a 7% advantage over the player. To this must be added the advantage accruing to the bank in the event of a tie, so the advantage to the bank is probably 10%, if not more. The vast majority of the suckers who frequent casinos don't have anything even remotely resembling an even break, and yet they persist in returning time and time again to fill the pockets of the casino owners.

I took up my position at the table that night and Kerry Packer made his appearance, a tall, powerfully-built young man who gave me an affable nod as he took up a place with two companions at the table facing me. The pit boss wheeled in a little trolley laden with sealed packs of cards, four of which were examined and opened by one of the Packer party. The decks were shuffled by me one by one, then cut by Packer and inserted into the shoe. Play began very conservatively. The bets were of a few hundred dollars at first, rising to perhaps a thousand on Packer's good cards. As the cards were dealt from the shoe and taken out of the game at the finish of a hand his companions would make notes on a sheet of paper. Packer took no wild chances, he stood pat on a six and allowed chance to dictate the outcome of a hand. At the end of an hour's play or so the house had won a few thousand dollars, but as the cards in the shoe diminished, so did Packer's bets increase, and so did the intervals in his deciding whether or not to ask for another card. At times he seemed to throw discretion to the winds and double or treble his bet in asking for a third card, and his winning hands began by far to exceed his losing ones. His bets increased to huge proportions. $50,000 on the initial two cards, a third card asked for and another $50,000 staked on it and so on. These bets were always preceded by enquiring glances between Packer and his companions, to be followed by almost imperceptible affirmative or negative movements of the head. Three times or so out of four the bank would lose on these bets. I played according to the book. Stand on a six, draw on anything less, and hope for the law of averages to give me the advantage, yet more often than not the bank would lose. I became stiff with tension and signalled to the pit bosses who had gathered to view this phenomenon that I required a break. A relief man took my place and I retired for fifteen minutes to recoup my energies.

News of Packer's phenomenal betting spread like wildfire throughout the casino, and the spectators stacked themselves ten deep around the table, a gasp escaping them as the imperturbable Australian pushed pile after pile of chips onto the baize surface. After four hours of play the card shoe was empty and Packer had won the amazing sum of $600,000 at my baccarat table. He gave me a nod of the head, shook my hand and pushed $6,000 of chips across the table to me.

'A tip for the dealer.'

Those were the only words he had uttered all during that fantastic session. The explanation, of course, was that Packer and his two companions had taken note of the cards already dealt, and being possessed of phenomenal memory, could predict with a degree of accuracy what card was likely to come out next from the remaining cards in the shoe. The win of course was tremendous publicity for the casino, whose clientele at the baccarat tables increased dramatically in the hope of emulating Packer's feat. However, to cut down on the chances of another such occurrence, the baccarat game at the Grand Nassau became one of a six-deck shoe, which would have required the brain of a computer to beat.

A couple of days later I happened to meet my Chevalier companion Mario, who had also accepted the Bahamas offer and was dealing at the Lido Casino on Paradise Island. The night before he had dealt at a private baccarat session reserved by Packer. The Australian had not been so lucky at that session. His winnings had come to only $450,000.

In later years I was to hear more and more about Kerry Packer and his legendary exploits in the gambling world. In the 1980s he is reported to have won $26 million at the MGM Grand in Las Vegas playing blackjack for $200,000 a hand, six hands at a time. During the same visit to Las Vegas they say he lost $13 million of those winnings in Caesar's Palace four days later. Mr Packer was also reported to have suffered the biggest losses ever sustained in gambling in the UK in September 1999, when he dropped £11 million in one night at Crockford's casino in London. And they say that such a sum is only a tiny fraction of his total wealth.

Packer is also reported to be incredibly generous when the fancy takes him. A story goes that when a waitress stayed on after closing time in a cafeteria to serve him a snack he asked her why she was working so late at night. To keep my kids and pay the mortgage, was her answer. A few days later she received a note from her bank telling her that a Mr Packer had paid off her loan, and that the title deeds to her home would follow in due time. These stories may be just stories and nothing else, I don't know. Gambling stories, with their accounts of vast sums won and lost, are prone to exaggeration. What I do know and can swear to is that Kerry Packer won $600,000 at my Nassau Grand baccarat table, and tipped me $6,000. Unfortunately for me, however, not all of that generous gift made its way into my pocket. House rules in most casinos are that all tips must be pooled and shared with all the staff.

SEVEN

THE ISLE OF MAN

Eighteen months are not very long in passing, and my contract in the Bahamas seemed to come up for renewal in no time at all. I had paid three visits to the family in Glasgow during that period, and although Rose was quite happy about the extra money I had been sending home and had put much of it away in savings, I was not at all happy at such a long separation from her and from the kids. In Glasgow I had a working life and a family life. I did my shifts at the casinos and then I could enjoy myself with Rose and the kids and with the odd night or two out in the company of my old pals. In Nassau, life consisted of a long and boring trek between hotel and casino and sun-drenched beach with no one you could really call a friend.

You might not think it possible to get fed up with a sun-bathed life of luxury living in a palatial hotel, surrounded by every conceivable amenity and rubbing shoulders with the famous and the wealthy, but my Nassau environment was so far removed from what I considered to be the real world that many were the times when I wished myself back in a Maryhill tenement, surrounded by the rough-and-ready, down-to-earth people I had grown up with. I missed my regular weekend visits to the pub for a drink with my old mates, and the heated arguments about the latest Celtic and Rangers match; I missed the regular visits to the Garrioch club where I boxed and sparred and trained a bit to keep myself fit, and above all I missed the wife and kids. After my late shifts in the Nassau Grand I used to go for long walks along the warm sandy beach, to breathe in the scented velvety air, and to wind down from the tensions of the gaming rooms before getting to bed. You might think it daft of me, but often during those walks I wished I were stepping out from the Chevalier into a cold and wet and windswept Buchanan Street in the middle of the night, looking for a taxi to take me home.

At the end of my eighteen months contract I took leave of the many working acquaintances I had made, and booked my flight home as quickly as I could. Rose was over the moon to have me back, and I rested up for a week or so, played around with the kids and drank numerous pints of Guinness with my mates at the local pub. I even paid a visit one Saturday afternoon to Firhill to see Partick Thistle play the Rangers and ate a hot pie at half time. They were still VC pies, I was told, but my taste buds must have changed, for they tasted awful.

I began thinking about starting work again, but now that I had been home for a few weeks I began to consider things realistically. There was a job for me at the Stakis casinos if I wanted, of that I was pretty sure, but that meant a significant drop in earnings, especially now that a no-tipping policy had been introduced there. The family had become accustomed to the big money I was sending home, and that had to be taken into consideration, especially since another addition to the family had recently arrived, this time a daughter, Lorraine. So I had the usual long discussion with Rose. Should I get in touch with the Bahamas people with a view to extending my contract for another 18 months, or should I stay home and carry on with the Glasgow casinos, even at much less than the rate I had been earning in the Nassau Grand? I didn't relish the idea of substantially reducing my income, and that aspect of it had to be thought about very hard.

Once again chance played a part in my decision. One night I was having a drink in Lauder's, just a few yards along from the Chevalier, and happened to bump into an old friend, Jack Clancy, a dealer I had worked with for a few months in the Regency. We chit-chatted for a while, and in between beers compared experiences. He had stayed on at the Regency until recently, and from his accounts the place didn't seem to have changed much. I mentioned my dilemma to him. Should I go back for another stint in the Bahamas or should I set my mind at rest and continue to work in the Glasgow area? I had no doubt at all that a job with the Stakis casinos would be forthcoming. Maybe I've said this before, but I considered myself to be as good as any other croupier in the business, and better than some. Moreover I had acquired a reputation for being 100% reliable, with never a day off during my time at the Chevalier and Regency, and had always been willing to stand in at other Stakis casinos when the need had arisen. I just could not screw up enough nerve to make a decision. My pal came up with a third possibility for me to consider. He was on a week's holiday at the moment, he explained, and had been dealing on Mediterranean cruise ships as an employee of the Lido casino in Douglas on the Isle of Man. He described the set-up to me. Since the Isle of Man was such a popular holiday resort attracting holidaymakers from all over the UK, the Lido casino worked to capacity during the summer, but closed its doors in the winter, when the island was all but deserted apart from the locals. During the winter months the management took over the running of the floating casinos set up on some of the cruise ships, staffed them with its own dealers and offered free winter Mediterranean cruises to many of its heavy-spending punters. These cruises sailed from Douglas, called in at all the big tourist ports in the Med, and lasted for a month at a time. The pay was not as much as I had been making in the Bahamas, but it was substantially more than I would have made in Glasgow, and according to my pal the tips were far in excess of what we used to make back in the Regency days. The cruises went on for six months, there was a week's paid holiday at the end of each cruise, and the Lido was in the market for experienced dealers.

On the strength of that information I stood him a drink and went home to see what Rose had to say about it. Somewhat to my surprise she did not give me an argument. As far as she was concerned, it seemed a perfectly good arrangement. The money was better than I would be getting in Glasgow, and I would be at home at the end of each month to give a hand with the kids. Some years back before I was married I had gone to the Isle of Man with some pals for a weekend to take in the TT motorbike races and I remembered it as being a very attractive place. I phoned the number Jack had given me, introduced myself and two days later I picked up a plane ticket left for me at Renfrew airport. Soon I was sitting in a very bumpy old Fokker Friendship prop plane on my way to an interview at the Lido casino.

I arrived at the fairly rudimentary airport at Castletown, then made my way to the Lido in Douglas. The two chaps who interviewed me asked me the usual questions. Where had I worked? How much experience did I have? Had I ever dealt on a floating casino? They then gave me particulars about the job. It was more or less as Jack Clancy had described it. I was to work in the Lido until it closed for the winter, then I would be assigned to a casino on board a cruise ship. The rules were as in any other casino, with something added on. The dealers were not to mix with the cruise passengers, and were not allowed ashore at any of the ports visited during the cruise. Each cruise lasted for a month, at the end of which I would be due a week's paid leave. The salary would be paid in sterling, but since the Lido and the cruise ships were registered in the Cayman Islands, my pay check would be drawn on a Cayman Islands bank and there would be no deduction for tax. I presented my CV, and gave the Stakis casinos and the Bahamas Gambling Commission as references. It took a lot of courage to get back onto that rickety old Fokker Friendship for the trip back to Glasgow, but I got there, shaken but safe, and waited.

Jack had filled me in about the background of the Lido. I like to know who I am working for, who the names are behind the superficial razzamataz and glitter of the casinos, so I did some homework in the Mitchell Library and looked up the back issues of the *Daily Express* where Jack had told me I could read up on all the publicity the Lido and its sister casino the Colony Club in London had been geting in the tabloid newspapers during my stay in the Bahamas. George Raft, the Hollywood actor, was one of the owners of the Douglas Lido, and his manager, Dino Cellini, was rumoured to be a close friend of Myer Lansky, the man with his fingers dug well into the gambling joints of Florida, Cuba and the Bahamas. This was at the time when George Raft, who had just opened the Colony Club, had had his British visa revoked by Roy Jenkins, the British Home Secretary, on the grounds that he, Raft, was an associate of known criminals. The papers were full of the affair, and George Raft had been interviewed at length by a reporter on the *Daily Express*.

'Somebody must have put the finger on me', said Raft, in answer to the reporter's questions. 'They haven't accused me of anything; they've just barred me from the country without any charges. I suppose somebody must have told them I have connections, but I'm not a member of any mob, never was. Sure, I know a lot of people who are connected. What am I to do when these guys come up and say hello to me—tell them to get lost? Sure I worked the speakeasies in my old dancing days. So they were owned by the mob, so what? So were all the joints where you could get work then. Was I supposed to starve? In my time I met them all: Al Capone, Joe Adonis, Frank Costello, Vito Genovese, Dutch Schultz, Myer Lansky, Lucky Luciano. They were all around when I was a young guy working the circuit. So maybe some of them were not the best of citizens, but they paid me good wages for honest work. What's wrong with that? This visa thing is just an excuse to get rid of me. The local mobs over there don't want me to get a piece of the action, they want it all themselves. Do you know that one club alone, in London, cleared $4.2 million last year? There's plenty for everybody, but they just don't want me in, so they pull a few strings and I'm out. I lead a quiet life. I mind my own business. I give work to lots of people. I don't ask for any trouble, I don't get in any fights. My slate's clean. I've never done time. If liking broads is an offence, then all right, but that's all I plead guilty to.'

This was in 1965. George Raft was 71 years old at the time.

I began to have second thoughts. It was all right to work for a legitimate operation like Stakis, and in the Bahamas it was the government who paid my wages, but with such a dodgy background what kind of security did I have if the group that ran the Lido and the cruises folded up? Anyhow I said nothing to Rose about what I had found out, put all doubts to the back of my mind and when I was told to report to the Lido in Douglas I packed my bags and got ready to present myself for work. No Fokker Friendship flight this time though. My stomach had still to recover from the last flight, so I took a train to Liverpool and the ferry from there to Douglas. I don't know what was worse, the flight or the sea crossing to the Isle of Man on the heavy seas that seemed to me to be tossing the ferryboat around like a cork. It was then I began to worry about the cruise ships and seasickness, and I hoped they were going to be a little more stable than the ferryboat.

The cruises were not due to start for another few weeks yet, so I was put to work right away at the Lido. The casino was more or less like any other place I had worked in Scotland. Give or take some difference in décor, casinos the world over are basically the same. Some roulette tables, some card tables, a couple of crap tables and that was it, so when you have worked one you've worked them all. By experience I could now tell by looking at the quality of the furnishings what type of punter you were going to cater for. The plusher the curtains, the deeper the carpet and the heavier the chandelier the wealthier the punter and the bigger the bets. I would have put the Lido in about the middle range of casinos. I suppose that after the glamour and glitter of the Bahamas anything would have looked a little bit drab, so I found the atmosphere at the Lido somewhat subdued and the customers not very inspiring. After the $20,000 bets and more that I had become accustomed to handling in the Nassau Grand, the five and ten pound bets I was covering hardly thrilled me. The season was coming to an end and the casino was about to close for the winter, the high rollers had gone to ground and the holidaymakers who came in for a quick flutter were thin on the floor and shallow in the pocket. There is nothing quite as boring as standing at an empty baccarat table shuffling and reshuffling a deck of cards and trying to look occupied, or trying to look enthusiastic when some young punter still wet behind the ears makes a big flourish with a ten pound bet to impress the girlfriend. I was glad when I was told to report to the cruise ship *Oceana*.

EIGHT

THE OCEANA

The *Oceana*, the cruise ship I had been assigned to, was literally a floating five star hotel and more. The area around and on the deck was the only place where the passenger was allowed to feel that he was on board a ship. Below decks, the width of the staircases and corridors, the plush carpets, the spaciousness and magnificent décor of the lounges and dining rooms, the opulence of the more expensive cabins, all these could not have been surpassed by anything a land-based five-star hotel had to offer. As was only to be expected, the gaming rooms were every bit as luxurious, with deep, soft carpets, heavy velvet drapes and walls covered by pink-tinged mirrors which gave a warm reflection to the light from the ornate crystal chandeliers. Everything was designed to instil euphoria in the mind of the punter, so as to lessen the pain of being separated from his money.

Nothing much, however, had been done to lessen the pain of the dealers who worked the casino. The money was certainly very good. The ship was registered in the Cayman Islands, so technically that was our place of employment and our income was tax free, but that barely made up for the conditions in which we had to operate for the month's duration of each cruise. We were considered to be members of the crew and shared their quarters, which, although adequate, were in no way comparable in amenity to what even the cheapest of the passenger cabins offered in the way of accommodation. For the passengers, in anything but the very roughest of seas, there was no sensation of being on board a ship—no roll, no vibration, no throb of engines. The crew cabins, each with two bunks, were well down in the bowels of the ship, and in them there could be no mistake as to what our environment was. You could just as well have been in a submarine. The throb of engines was ever-present, the circulated air smelled of machine oil and the tiny en suite shower and toilet cubicle made gurgling and sucking noises all night, and if your companion happened to be a snorer or given to other bodily noises, that really topped things off. I used my cabin simply as a place to sleep, and although the dealer who shared it with me was a reasonable enough type from London who washed and didn't suffer too much from flatulence, by mutual consent we always tried to work different shifts so as to have the cabin to ourselves at rest times. This wasn't too difficult to arrange. The gaming rooms worked for nearly 15 hours a day, from midday to 6 in the afternoon and from 9pm till 6 o'clock next morning, and if you spoke nicely to the casino manager he usually tried to make up the shifts to suit. He knew the problems of two men sleeping together at the same time in such a small space, so he did his best to arrange things accordingly. A contented and well-rested squad of croupiers, after all, makes for a contented gaming room and for fewer slips at the tables.

Unlike the members of the crew who dealt directly with the passenger's needs, we had a further disadvantage. We were effectively segregated from the paying customers and in no circumstances were we allowed to mix with them. A small section of a lower deck, well out of sight of the passengers, was set aside for our exercise area, and that was the only space we had to go to for a breath of sea air and for a change from either the suffocating luxury of the gaming rooms or the claustrophobia of our cabins. Even here we couldn't get away from the sight of playing cards. This area was set aside for the below decks crews also, and would they not bring out their dog-eared packs of cards hoping to coax us into a game so as to get some ideas from the experts, as we were supposed to be! Once at your place of work, however, you could have been in the gaming room of any land-based casino, the main difference being that your punters did not vary as much as they did on land, where you might get a good percentage of casual visitors. Of the two thousand or so cruise passengers, possibly half were there for the cruise only and never visited the casino. The rest were there for the thrill of gambling on the high seas and the opportunity to visit the casinos at the various ports of call, and we were required to deal to the same faces day after day.

Cheesed off with being segregated from the paying customers, I began to make myself familiar with the geography of the ship. I explored every labyrinthine passage in the vicinity of the engine room, climbed up and down narrow metal stairways and through narrow corridors, until I found a small service door which gave onto a remote corner of the upper passenger deck. This road discovered, now and then I would change into appropriate togs and mix freely for a time with the paying customers, behind the disguise of a heavy pair of sunglasses and a different hair parting to the one I wore on the casino floor. I enjoyed these illicit excursions thoroughly at first, without ever giving a thought to what might have been my punishment if I had been found out. After a while though, these trips began to pall. It was a lot of bother to change clothes and hair style just for the sake of a walk with the toffs, and I gave it up after half a dozen tries.

The casino managers did not take kindly to the idea of their customers going into other betting centres at the various ports of call, where money won on the cruise might be lost without the ship casino having the chance of winning it back, nor did they relish the thought that some high-rolling gambler, having been provided with free transportation by the cruise ship for the privilege of getting there, might lose all his or her money at some foreign casino. To the cruise organisers, these considerations are of secondary importance. The ports of call are chosen to make the cruise as attractive as possible for everyone on board, and since almost all of the most sought-after ports of call have casinos, the ship casino management just have to accept that fact and hope that as little money as possible is lost by punters while on land.

The money that was poured out on these cruises was incredible. The bare cost of the cruise itself could range from a couple of thousand pounds to as much as twenty thousand, depending on the location of the cabins. This was a lot of money, bearing in mind that we are talking of 1968 or so. Over and above that, the money spent on board ship and during the visits ashore was staggering. The ship provided banking facilities, where letters of credit and certified cheques for many hundreds of thousands of pounds were changed every day of the cruise. The ubiquitous credit card one sees nowadays was not in common use as yet. Some of the passengers would come on board with suitcases stuffed with cash, and would present themselves at the tables with briefcases full of £20 and £50 notes, which dwindled steadily during the course of a night's or a day's play. A busy roulette table could make a profit of £100,000 or so each session, a baccarat or blackjack table could win possibly £30,000 or £50,000 and a crap table the same.

On each cruise you had half a dozen or so professional gamblers. Although one or two of them had worked out elaborate systems to try out on the roulette tables and would spend hours and considerable sums of money in the hope of beating the odds, the majority of them confined themselves to the card tables, where skill plays a big part in the betting process. Some of the professional types confined themselves to the poker games, poker being the game where experience and skill counts for the most. A professional gambler makes his living playing cards and plays the percentages. He does not look for a massive win, although all nourish the hope of someday drawing an unbeatable hand of cards at some dreamt-of no-limit game. A massive win also admits of the possibility of a massive loss, and few gamblers have the stomach to risk such disasters. The run-of-the-mill professional gambler is satisfied with playing for relatively modest stakes and depends on his skill and nerve to bring him a profit. A good professional will always beat a good amateur, and there are plenty of good hopeful amateurs with money to burn waiting to be plucked clean.

The poker games were played in private rooms hired out to the players together with the services of a dealer for about £500 per hour. When you think that some of these sessions could last for as long as ten hours it gives some idea of the profits made by the house. It did not tax my powers of mental arithmetic to figure out that on a month's cruise the house would probably clear about £6 million in profit. No wonder that all kinds of inducements were offered to clients to tempt them on board. Elegant rooms, spectacular entertainment in the nightly cabarets, free drinks and cigarettes while gambling and the presence of willing females only too eager to make the punter forget his losses or celebrate his winnings by sharing his bed at night. All for free, but in the case of the last mentioned perk, a large tip, commensurate with the quality of the 'merchandise' and with the expertise of the service provided, is expected and always given.

The *Oceana*'s first stop after leaving Douglas was at Estoril in Portugal, where the famous Casino Internacional was a Mecca for the gamblers on board. The ship anchored in the bay for two days, then sailed on through the Gibraltar Straits and north to Barcelona for another two day's stop. Then on to Nice and Cannes for a similar break, followed by a circular tour of the Med, calling at Monte Carlo, San Remo in Italy then to Corfu and Greece. It was at these ports of call that I felt a complete prisoner on the ship. Unlike the rest of the crew the croupiers and other casino workers were not allowed ashore, and it was galling to be denied a visit to the legendary casinos at these resorts. The management did not want any contact between us and the passengers, for fear, I suppose, that we might cook up some cheating scam or other with the casino customers. I just did not see the logic of this. On land no restriction was ever placed on the connections or friendships we might strike up with casino customers, where the same danger existed for the management, so why on earth were we not allowed to rub shoulders with the paying customers on a cruise? As though cheating on anybody's part in a casino is easy. It is not, unless everyone—the dealers, the inspectors and the pit bosses—are all in the scam together.

An inspector worth his salt should be able to pick up a dishonest dealer immediately. A winning streak at a card table does not go long unnoticed. The inspector knows what to look for. Is the winning streak pure chance or is there some scam involved? Is a dealer allowing his cards to be glimpsed by

an onlooker, who in turn is signalling the lucky player? By a repetitious movement of fingers, or of hands or of any part of the body, is a signal being sent by
the dealer directly to the player? Without the involvement of the dealer, have
the cards been marked in any way, a corner slightly bent on one card, a faint
scratch on the back of another? Is the punter on a winning streak wearing
tinted glasses of some sort, so as to be able to pick up chemical markings put
on several key cards which cannot be seen in normal light? If there are any
onlookers at a game, is there one who moves around behind the players, perhaps taking note of their hands and signalling an accomplice player? At the
roulette table are late bets being properly announced and the correct number
identified?

At a crap table have the house dice been surreptitiously changed by the
crap dealer with a loaded set, so as to favour one particular player? Has the
player himself deceived the dealer and switched dice? An alert and suspicious
inspector or pit boss would immediately snatch up the suspected dice and
examine them carefully. The dice used in casinos are opaque and usually of a
reddish colour with white dots, and any attempt to substitute them with a
loaded set can easily be detected by holding the suspect dice up to a light
source for examination. If the loading on the dice has been skilfully inserted
under or in the dot and cannot be detected by the light test, then six or so rolls
of the dice can determine whether the same number always comes up, an occurrence so far outwith normal odds that further investigation is warranted. If
the inspectors and pit bosses are worth their salt, then cheating at any particular table will not last for any length of time.

A cheating scam which has gone into legend amongst dealers was one attempted at a Florida hotel in the 1950s against Nick 'the Greek' Dandalos, the
famous international gambler. The game, poker, was played at the poolside
with the Greek's back to the high-rise hotel behind and with a dealer supplied
by the hotel casino in charge of the table. In one of the hotel rooms, high and
slightly to the side of the gaming table, an accomplice was observing the Greek's
cards through high-powered binoculars and sending information by short wave
radio to a hearing aid in the opponent's ear. Two or three hands were won in
this way, until the astute dealer noticed that before making a decision, the
crooked gambler invariably touched his hearing aid. He was able to alert the
house, and hotel detectives, having identified the source of the signal, burst
into the room, discovered the binoculars and radio equipment and arrested
both men, who were immediately blacklisted from every casino in the country. Ian Fleming, who was in Florida at the time, read of the case in the papers
and incorporated the incident into his James Bond novel, *Goldfinger*. The scene

was enacted in the film of that name, with Sean Connery being cheated by the villain Gert Frobe at a poolside game. Connery realises what is happening and turns the tables on the villain. For the sake of dramatic impact, in the film the accomplice was portrayed as a beautiful woman who is killed by Goldfinger for her failure.

I found the ban on going ashore annoying, to say the least. I had of course been informed about this ban before taking the job, but I had not realised just how frustrating it was going to be having to sit on our postage stamp of a deck and see the likes of Cannes, Nice and the legendary Monte Carlo just a few yards away and not to be able to set foot in these places. At the end of my first cruise, with five more to go, I was already resolved not to seek a renewal of contract.

The next five months were as long and as boring as any I have ever spent. The same confined area of the ship, the same tiny cabin, the same restricted deck area, the same tantalising view of the famous places that were out of bounds to us, the same parade of faces at the gaming tables, all added up to a prison sentence to be served with as much patience as possible. The one welcome break was the week's visit to Glasgow at the end of each cruise. To be with Rose and the kids and to walk the familiar streets of Glasgow with them on dreich winter days was a tonic which made the following month's confinement bearable. Rose and I talked a lot about the future, and we came to the conclusion that I should apply for my old job back with the Stakis casinos and make a career of it there. We now had enough money put aside to ensure that the kids could stay on at school if they were able and wanted to. I was determined to make sure that they would have the chance of the education that I never had. I had no doubt whatsoever that I could walk back into my old place at the Chevalier. I knew everything there was to know about the game; I had stood in several times for the inspector and once for the pit boss himself, and these jobs are not given to someone who doesn't have the full confidence of the management.

However, during the course of the final cruise I became aware of two American types who spent hours in the casino, sauntering casually from table to table, making small bets and obviously taking note of everything going on around them. My mind went back two or three years to the Chevalier and to the Bahamas casino scouts. These two were clones of the ones who had offered me a job in the Bahamas. They were conservatively dressed in well-cut dark suits, with white shirts and ties to match, and they moved about on the floor with their movements almost synchronised. The word 'scout' was written large all over them, and before long the two were the main topic of conversation amongst the casino staff. Two American casino scouts were on board. The news spread, but they made no approach to anyone during the four weeks of the cruise. If they had we wouldn't have been able to talk to them anyhow, given that contact with the passengers was not allowed, but on the last day of the cruise one of them, after playing a few hands and losing a few pounds worth of chips at my baccarat table, offered me his card. Written on the back of it was the name of a hotel in Douglas.

'Glad to have seen you,' he said. 'By now you've probably guessed what we do. Please get in touch as soon as you can at this hotel. I'm sure you will be interested in what we have to offer.'

The name on the card I remember well.

> Douglas Madden, Representative,
> *Operator Providers Inc.*

There was an address in San Diego, and on the back the pencilled number of a Douglas hotel.

Once disembarked at Douglas, I made a hurried phone call to Rose and told her that I would be delayed for a day on the Isle of Man, with explanations to come later, which did not please her at all. I then phoned Douglas Madden at his hotel. Two hours later I was sitting in the hotel lounge in the company of three other dealers, one from the *Oceana*, one from a casino in Barcelona and another who had come all the way from a casino in San Remo, one of the ports of call. We listened to the scouts' sales pitch.

They represented an agency for the supply of dealers and croupiers on request to casinos in the western states of the USA. We would be supplied with accommodation in Las Vegas and would be employed by them and assigned as needed to various casinos, principally in Las Vegas but in other cities if the need arose. We would be answerable to the management of whatever casino we were assigned to, but our wages would be paid by the agency and our work contract would be with them. I could see the Adam's apples of my three companions bobbing frantically up and down when the amount we were to be paid was mentioned. I'm sure I was swallowing quickly as well, for the sum mentioned was well in excess of what I had been earning in the Bahamas, although tax would have to be paid on it. We asked a few questions and left with a handshake and a request for an answer within three days.

The next day I was on a train from Liverpool to Glasgow, rehearsing over and over again what I would have to say to convince Rose that I should take the offer, for mentally I had accepted the job as soon as it was offered to me. Las Vegas! The Mecca of gamblers! The playground of the Hollywood stars and the American Mafia! Or so I thought. All the films I had seen about the place, such as *Ocean's Eleven* and *Viva Las Vegas*, came to mind, and although I was no longer the naïve Maryhill boy who went open-mouthed to the cinema when he could dig up the money to watch Humphrey Bogart and Edward G. Robinson in movies about gangsters and gambling, the idea of spending some time in the legendary Las Vegas and being paid handsomely for doing so was irresistible. The glamour attached to that name! One or two of my work mates in the Stakis casinos had worked there and used to speak enthusiastically about their experiences. Not a place they would want to spend their lives in, they used to say, but definitely a place to see and work in for a while. You couldn't call yourself a dealer unless you had experienced the likes of Binion's Horseshoe and Goodman's Nite Spot in downtown Vegas. No fancy hotel nonsense about places like that, they said. Just honest, down-to-earth gambling joints with punters the likes of which you had never seen in your life before, and bets and poker games you could only dream about. Harking back to the stories I used to hear whetted my appetite.

I hadn't realised that it was going to be so difficult to convince Rose, however. I kept stressing the fact of the big money I would be making compared to what I would get going back to the Stakis organisation. I would be home every three months, I said. The contract would only be for two years and then definitely I would come back to Glasgow for good, honest I would. It was purely for the good of the family, I kept repeating. I knew it was hard for her looking after the three kids on her own, but it would be only for a few years and then we would all get the benefit of the extra money that would be coming in. Finally, after hours of persuasion, but very, very reluctantly, Rose agreed.

NINE

LAS VEGAS

I n all, four British dealers had been recruited by the agency scouts, myself and three others from London clubs. As I sat with them on the Heathrow-Boston-Los Angeles flight I began thinking of what lay ahead of me. I had done my homework on Las Vegas in the Mitchell Library my old Ruchill paint shop foreman John McCluskey had introduced me to, and after poring over all the references I could find about Nevada and Las Vegas, my head was brimming over with facts and figures about the place where I would be dealing and working the wheel for the next two years.

Las Vegas stands at an altitude of 2,033 feet, in the middle of a desert in the southern part of the state of Nevada. Mormons from Utah were the first settlers in the area as they went west along the old Spanish trail in search of land they could take over as their own, attracted there by stories of the abundant water the Spanish had found from artesian wells in the middle of the desert. They found these wells, which supply water to Las Vegas to this day, and set up a settlement in the shallow valley to which the Spanish had given the name 'Las Vegas' (The Meadows).

In 1864 the US Army was attracted to the site and built Fort Baker there, whereupon the Mormons, who had been in search of a land which they could develop according to their own religious beliefs, uncontaminated by the outside world, moved out and eventually built their Camelot further north in Salt Lake City. They left behind a ramshackle collection of buildings, soon to be taken over by bands of wandering prospectors who mined the sparse deposits of gold and silver in the area. In 1905 a railroad was built to join Fort Baker with Los Angeles. At the end of the twenties, in the years of the great economic depression, the Nevada state legislature passed a law legalising gambling, hoping to attract revenue for the undeveloped state, and gambling houses licensed by them were opened up in two settlements, Reno in the north and Las Vegas in the south. Although Reno was a sizeable town with one or two fairly well appointed hotels with casinos attached, Las Vegas was strictly a one-horse two-track railway junction cowboy town, whose only customers were the soldiers stationed at the nearby Fort Baker, and any addicted gambler willing to put up with the fairly basic motel accommodation to be found there. For years the population of the town remained static at about 5,000 inhabitants.

Then, in the 1930s, two events took place that were to give birth to the Las Vegas we know today. A huge dam, the biggest in the world then, was built across the Black Canyon of the Colorado River at the Nevada-Arizona border. Originally called Boulder Dam, it was renamed the Hoover Dam in honour of the president who authorised its construction, and created one of the largest man-made lakes ever seen, Lake Mead. The waters from it provided cheap and limitless electricity to several of the western states of America, and made possible the incandescent sea of neon that lights up the modern Las Vegas. Electricity in Nevada is cheaper than water and in some establishments is literally never switched off. Any one of the super hotels that go to make up the Vegas of today consumes as much electricity as is used up by whole towns of 50,000 to 60,000 inhabitants.

The second of these events was in 1937, when a certain Bugsy Siegel appeared on the scene. Siegel was a New York gangster with a string of murders and other miscellaneous crimes to his name. In New York he had worked for both Lucky Luciano and Myer Lansky, the two notorious East Coast gangsters, and had been sent to Los Angeles to extend the New York crime syndicate's activities to the West Coast. There he opened a string of illegal gambling dens and off-shore gambling ships. Hearing of the legal gambling that was allowed in Nevada, just 300 miles from Los Angeles, he made use of the newly opened motor road which now joined the two places and drove to Las Vegas to inspect the set-up there. He was struck by the potential of the place, ramshackle and primitive though it was by Los Angeles standards.

The town had all the makings of a golden opportunity, he reasoned. Ever since the imprisonment of Al Capone on tax evasion charges ten years before, the gang bosses lived in fear of the taxman. The local police could be bribed to turn a blind eye to illegal activities, and local officials could be bought off, but the federal government was untouchable, and in the Capone case had found the one sure weapon to be used against organised crime—prosecution for income tax evasion. The crime bosses thought of every possible way in which they could launder the vast stream of money flowing in from their various rackets and put it away safe from prosecution. It had been calculated by a special investigator, Elliot Ness, the federal agent who had finally brought Capone to justice, that the money handled by the crime syndicates was as great as the combined cash flow of the all motor car manufacturers of America put together, and not one penny of tax was paid on it. With gambling legal in Las Vegas, and access to it from the Los Angeles area now easy because of the new road, Bugsy Siegel reasoned that a luxury hotel with an attached casino would be a great attraction to the wealthy set of Southern California, and that a string of such complexes could provide the perfect front for the laundering of a great deal of the syndicate's dirty money. Moreover, there was talk of building a commercial airport nearby, and that would help to provide easy access for visitors from all over the country.

Siegel lost no time and approached Lansky with his idea, who, after a visit to Las Vegas, became as enthusiastic as Siegel about the plan. However, such a hotel casino project would cost millions upon millions of dollars, much too much for one man alone to risk. Lansky decided to offer participation in the plan to the crime syndicate, and in order to discuss the matter a conference of all the crime families of the US was held in Havana, a place guaranteed to be safe from the prying eyes and ears of the FBI. Agreement was reached, each crime family was to provide an equal amount of capital, and an offshore company with fictitious shareholders was set up to launch the project.

Siegel had already been busy consulting with architects and suppliers, and had come up with a figure of $4 million for the building of the hotel, a huge sum in those days. That sum proved to be very much underestimated and the backers in the syndicate found themselves having to pour more and more money into the project, until $6 million had been spent, with no date in sight for the completion of the hotel-casino. Suspicions were aroused that Siegel was creaming money off the building contracts and hiding it in the Cayman Islands, in bank accounts in the name of his film star mistress Virginia Hill, but even though these suspicions were found to be based on fact, the syndicate decided to allow him to carry on until the hotel was up and running, since any immediate action would further delay the project.

The Flamingo, as the hotel was named, was the first of the many luxury hotel-casinos that were to make Las Vegas the gambling capital of the world and a Mecca for millions of tourists each year. It opened with a grand flourish on Boxing Day 1946, with what was the most spectacular event ever seen outside of Hollywood. Siegel employed the film star George Raft, who was no stranger to the gambling scene and well connected to many of the crime bosses, to act as his entertainment and publicity consultant, and gave him a small block of shares in the Flamingo as payment. The new hotel was the height of luxury and could have come straight from a Hollywood film set. The restaurant provided a menu prepared by a top chef imported from Quaglino's in

London, and the casino was staffed by croupiers and dealers poached from gambling houses in Havana and the Bahamas. George Jessel, a popular comedian of the day, performed as master of ceremonies at the gala opening, and dozens of Hollywood stars were invited for the occasion. Lana Turner, escorted by Johnny Stompanato, the Mafia hoodlum who was later to be stabbed to death by her daughter, made a grand entrance, as did Joan Crawford, Cesar Romero, Humphrey Bogart, Clark Gable, Robert Mitchum and others. Xavier Cugat and his orchestra provided the music. Jimmy Durante went into his 'Schnozzle' act, Abbot and Costello did theirs with assistance from the Three Stooges, and Frank Sinatra sang in the cabaret show.

The occasion was a brilliant success, and the casino showed a profit of $500,000 just for that one night, an absolute fortune in today's values. Bugsy's dream had been realised, but he had signed his own death sentence months before by taking money which by rights should have gone into the pockets of the Mob. Two weeks later, as he relaxed in the bungalow he shared with Virginia Hill in the grounds of the Flamingo, the postponed execution order was carried out. A fusillade of shots came through the living-room window, one of which hit Siegel in the eye, killing him instantly. His murder underlined the point he was fond of making when doubts were expressed by the Las Vegas city fathers about the wisdom of allowing Mob money into Vegas and the violence that might result: 'You don't have to worry a bit, we only kill each other!'

The city fathers' fears of possible Mob-related violence were somewhat difficult to understand, given that Las Vegas in those days had the biggest murder rate per head of population of any city in the US, with never a day passing without several shooting incidents in the streets and in the gambling joints.

The opening of the Flamingo marked the beginning of a building boom in Las Vegas and a change of image for the town. Old gambling joints along the main road, or the Strip, as the four-mile stretch of the Las Vegas boulevard was known, were torn down and huge hotel-casino complexes were built in their place. Until the coming of the Flamingo, gambling had taken place in dark smoky rooms where the dealers dressed in braces and shirtsleeves, sported green eye shades and as like as not wore a six-gun stuffed down the back of their trousers, but following the Flamingo example things began to change. As gambling began to acquire a veneer of respectability and glamour, legitimate money from banks and financial institutions began pouring in for investment, with the big hotel chains outdoing one another in the erection of gaudy and ostentatious gambling palaces. The big Hollywood film studios also participated in the boom, with MGM, Warner Brothers, Twentieth Century Fox and

Walt Disney all contributing to the row of neon-lit hotel-casinos which now lined the high street of Las Vegas. Federal funding helped in all this. The huge Boulder Dam, in the building of which 99 workers were killed, was now fully operational just 25 miles away, and provided an inexhaustible supply of electricity for the building boom. An atomic test site, the Nevada Flats, was opened a few hundred miles north of the city, Fort Baker was expanded into a huge military base, settlers flocked to the area and the permanent population of the city grew from 5000 in 1930 to 750,000 in 1965.

The atom bomb testing site on Nevada Flats attracted tourists in their thousands to the Las Vegas area. They wanted to be on hand to witness the testing of the new wonder bombs and caravan parks sprouted up overnight as thousands came to view the spectacle. About 50 miles from Las Vegas, the 4000-feet-high Mount Charleston became a favourite viewing spot, and since in those days the Atomic Commission gave prior notice of testings, thousands of spectators flocked to the high ground to watch. The flashes of light from the explosions could plainly be seen in the casinos, and some punters even started betting on when the next bomb would be exploded, the day of the week and the hour of the day. Literally hundreds of tests were carried out during the time Nevada Flats was in use, with never a thought given to the possible danger from the resulting fall-out. When the authorities at last became aware of the fatal consequences of exposure to radiation, the site was closed down and hundreds of square miles around it cordoned off. The Nevada-Arizona area, with its spectacular scenery, had been a favourite spot for the filming of Westerns, and John Ford filmed most of his John Wayne films within a couple of hundred miles downwind of Nevada Flats. It may be coincidence, but John Wayne, Ward Bond, Robert Ryan, Ben Johnson and Warren Oates, all actors who had made dozens of Westerns in the area, all died of cancer, as did John Ford himself and many of the production crews of those films. It must be assumed that many of these deaths were due to the radiation fall-out from the Nevada Flats atomic tests. It will never be known what damage was done to the thousands of spectators who came to witness the testing of the military's new weapon.

The murder of Bugsy Seigel had drawn the attention of the US government to the infiltration of organised crime into the state of Nevada, and in 1955 a change of state government resulted in an attempt to clean out the criminal elements. Slowly the control of the mobs over gambling in the state of Nevada was loosened. The city's growth surged in the mid-1950s as more casinos were built, and again in the mid-1960s when the industrialist Howard Hughes bought tracts of land on the Strip and opened his own hotel-casino complex, the Dunes Hotel, the first of several Hughes-owned establishments. Another economic boom began in the mid-1980s with the building of a new series of extravagant themed hotel-casino complexes with thousands of rooms, this time emphasizing family entertainment along the lines of the Disneyworld hotels. In these, the kids could play by the poolside and in amusement arcades under the supervision of child minders, and mom and pop could gamble to their heart's content and lose their shirts in the slot machines and gaming tables.

On arrival at Los Angeles airport we were met by a representative of the agency who introduced himself simply as 'Pete'. He informed us that since our scheduled flight to Las Vegas was subject to a long delay because of work to the runway there, he would be driving us the three hundred miles to our destination. We had arrived at Los Angeles at 9.30 in the morning and the temperature was already climbing into the seventies. By the time of our departure around noon it was nudging the eighty mark, and by the time we had reached the rim of the Nevada desert in the middle of the afternoon the thermometer had reached into the high nineties, but with the atmosphere appearing cleaner and sharper in marked contrast to the smog of the sprawling Los Angeles we had left behind.

I don't know what I had expected to find when eventually we drove along the highway into the outskirts of Las Vegas as dusk was falling. The approach to most towns or cities is heralded by the appearance of a few houses or factories, with the buildings growing ever denser as one approaches the town centre, but not so in Las Vegas. It must be the only town in the world which is approached, not through rows of buildings, but through mile after mile of gaudy electric and neon signs, which seem to be lit twenty-four hours a day. These spaghetti-like neon strips are suspended on metal frames signs and woven into shapes which make little sense when seen in daylight, but which at night reveal themselves as advertising for the countless attractions that lie in wait a few miles further along: cowboys spinning lariats, high-stepping, scantily-clad chorus girls, whirling roulette wheels, cascading playing cards and tumbling dice set against a background of floating dollar bills, lights flashing and exploding and coalescing into adverts for Coca-Cola, with Pepsi Cola signs matching them watt for watt.

Huge yellow McDonald's signs straddled the road with bridges created out of interwoven neon strips and vie with Kentucky Fried Chicken adverts in garishness. One huge sign in particular sticks in my mind. Above a long, low structure at the side of the road a sign proclaimed: 'Topless Pizza Parlour'. I couldn't imagine what a topless pizza was! Multi-coloured signs calling attention to the Dunes Casino, the Gold Nugget, the Sands, the Desert Inn, Kings High, One-Eyed Jacks and others appeared at the side of the highway. A huge neon Ben Hur chariot was driven by a Roman centurion through the illuminated portals of Caesar's Palace, flanked by huge posters depicting sexy Roman maidens serving drinks on Cleopatra's barge. Lights fashioned into the shape of an exploding atom bomb terminated in the name 'Silver Palace'. The names of entertainers shone forth in squares of revolving lights. Sinatra (no Frank necessary, the surname was enough) Dean Martin, King Cole, Rosemary Clooney, Sammy Davis, Louis Prima, Andy Williams, the Casa Loma Orchestra, each casino tried to outdo its neighbour in the entertainment offered free to entice the tourist through its portals to be fleeced of his or her money.

Our chauffeur kept up a running commentary as we drove slowly for some miles along this brilliantly-lit strip, pointing out what were to him famous places of interest, until finally we came to an intersection where the blaze of lights was like the inside of an iron furnace.

'Nothing like this anywhere else on earth. This is downtown Las Vegas.'

Pete repeated these words to us proudly several times. The main contributors to this blast of light were four buildings facing one another at the intersection of two roads, with the names Binion's Horseshoe, the Gold Nugget, the Fremont and the Four Queens spelled out in thousands upon thousands of watts of electricity. Here we turned left into Fremont Street, a comparatively dark thoroughfare with relatively modest signs advertising obscure girlie bars, poker clubs and keno parlours. Fremont Street ran at right angles to the main strip and contained casinos at every street corner. Low, rambling buildings with names like Goodman's Nite Spot, Four Jacks, and, on the opposite side of the street, Lucky Chance. Row upon row of girlie clubs with names like the Strip Casino, Bottoms Up and Kings High stretched as far as the eye could see. Double Zero flashed in and out, alternating with One-Eyed Jacks on the opposite side of the road.

Half a mile further along the street, all of it flanked by bars and nightclubs and poker saloons, we drove into the entrance of a large apartment block where Pete showed us to our respective apartments. The accommodation was spacious and well-appointed and stopped just short of being luxurious. Here the agency man left us with instructions to be ready the next day at noon, when we would be given our first assignments. He tossed us each two keys, one for the apartment and the other for one of the four cars parked at the condominium entrance. He shook our hands, wished us well and left us to our own resources.

TEN

THE SANDS

I had a pretty good idea what the Sands Hotel was going to look like even before I had been assigned to it as my first job in Las Vegas. The film *Ocean's Eleven* was still going the rounds in Glasgow when I had left for the Bahamas, and scenes from the film, with Sinatra and ten of his fellow ex-soldiers planning a robbery from five casinos in Las Vegas, with most of the action filmed in the Sands, were still fresh in my mind. During the production of the film Frank Sinatra, who took the leading part of Danny Ocean, the mastermind behind the robbery, with Dean Martin, Joey Bishop, Peter Lawford and Sammy Davies Jr, as four of his collaborators, worked on the film during the day and then performed in the Sands cabaret at night. The group had been given the name of Sinatra's Rat Pack. Once the film was finished they continued to make the Sands their stomping ground and often performed in the cabaret for the sheer pleasure of it. Because of the publicity given to the Sands by the film it had become the most famous of all the casinos on the Strip, replacing the Flamingo, which until then had occupied that position by reason of its Mob and Mafia origins.

The reality, however, was much more startling than I could have imagined. The brightly-lit entrance opened into a huge room filled with row upon row of slot machines, which produced a noise like the machine room of a busy factory as hundreds of players fed dollar after dollar into them. It was said at the time that there were 50,000 slot machines in Las Vegas, and it sounded to me as if they were all there in that one room in the Sands.

Ninety percent of the players at these machines were typical middle-American tourists, flown or bussed in for a week or a fortnight's gambling, the women with big hamburger bums and the men with steak-filled beer bellies. Some of the women wore a glove on their lever-pulling hand to save them from the blisters which would certainly have been caused by the incessant pulling if not protected. Almost all of them had large paper cups in their hands, filled with coins which they kept feeding into the slots. When empty, these cups were replenished at the casino cashier's desk and after another session of frantic lever-pulling were soon empty again. From time to time there would be a tinkling clatter of falling coins as a machine spewed out a jackpot, to be accompanied by shrieks of delight from some near-hysterical female winner too overcome by the delight of winning to realise that she had put in $100 to win $50. Some of these machines did pay out huge jackpots, $5,000 to $50,000, but the cynics said that the machines were fixed, and paid out the big money at preset times to casino employees posing as punters. These jackpots were paid out at peak customer periods, said some disgruntled losers, so as to encourage more and more punters to feed more and more dollars into the machines.

Even though it was only a fraction of the size of the main gaming area there were more guards in the slot-machine room than there were floor inspectors, or boxmen as the are called in the States, in the games room. They had to be on the constant look-out for thieves and pickpockets and would-be cheats, some of whom used ingenious methods to coax money from the one-armed bandits. Some employed powerful magnets in an attempt to stop the rollers at a winning position, although to foil such attempts machines with plastic gears and rollers were being introduced. Some had thin metal rods which they tried to insert between the glass and the metal of the window for the same purpose. Others came in small groups and surrounded a machine so as to block the view of any nearby inspector, before forcing open the back where the cash box was situated with a hidden hammer and chisel and then making a dash for the door with the loot. The machine they chose was invariably in the proximity of the exit, so as to make escape easier. To make escape as difficult as possible for an absconding thief or thieves, the entrance to the slot-machine room was made as narrow as safety regulations permitted. To compensate for this there was usually an overabundance of emergency fire exits, for it would have done the image of Las Vegas no good whatsoever if tourists were to be killed in a fire or some such emergency.

Today the slot machines are played by about 40 per cent of casino frequenters, the largest proportion of visitors to play any one game. It wasn't always so, since in the early days of gambling in Las Vegas the slot machines were not thought of as serious games of chance. They were indulged in for the most part by the wives whose husbands were in the main gambling rooms trying their luck at the card games and the roulette wheel. It was the introduction of video games that brought about changes in the old one-armed bandits and increased their popularity. A new line of machines, incorporating the vivid graphics and sound effects of the video games, was introduced by the slot machine manufacturers, and these spectacular effects attracted more and more addicts to them. The casino operators have added further refinements, such as connecting several machines together electronically, taking a small percentage of each play and adding it to a communal jackpot total. This total can now grow to a huge amount, incredibly into the millions, and although the odds against hitting this jackpot are immense, one lucky player will eventually win in a big way, thus attracting more and more addicts to this form of gambling. Nowadays a large proportion of a casino's profits comes from the new generation of one-armed bandits.

In a casino everybody is under surveillance. Since the players are there to win, some of them will try to cheat if they can, so the dealer or croupier has to watch them closely. The dealers and croupiers in turn are watched over by the boxmen, to make sure that they are not colluding with a player, and the boxmen in turn are scrutinised carefully by the pit bosses, who in turn are kept under close observation by the floor manager, who in turn is spied on by the general manager. Everything that happens on the casino floor is now monitored by closed-circuit TV cameras which can be made to zoom in on any suspicious activity at the tables. The video tapes from these cameras are carefully stored away for a time and are scrutinised for suspicious behaviour if any game is seen to be losing more than the natural odds allow for statistically. There can be no other workplace on earth where so much loose cash circulates so openly and casually, and there can be no other workplace in the world so closely monitored for signs of dishonesty on the part of the staff, or where retribution and punishment is as swift or as ruthless as that meted out on a Las Vegas casino floor. In European casinos punishment for cheating on the part of an employee is immediate dismissal and loss of his or her dealer's licence. I had it on very reliable hearsay that the desert on the outskirts of Las Vegas was littered with the graves of those employees who in the past were foolhardy enough to swindle their gangster bosses. If a punter was caught cheating he was courteously invited into the manager's office, where his fingers are broken or pounded with a heavy hammer, effectively putting him out of gambling action for quite some time.

From the strident cacophony of the slot-machine room a shallow staircase led up to the relatively peaceful gaming room which was much like any other gaming room in any other casino, with 6 roulette tables and about 12 other card and craps tables. Every casino in Vegas depends on the hordes of tourists who visit this gambling Disneyland, and the Sands had a special attraction for the visitor. Almost every night some well-known characters from the Hollywood studios could be seen trying their luck at the tables, and some-one from the Sinatra Rat Pack was sure to be there somewhere among the crowd.

Dean Martin usually came alone and favoured the baccarat tables. He didn't bet much, so he didn't lose much. He kept a low profile and stayed for long periods rooted to the one spot. He seemed to enjoy spending hours at the one table with a drink in his hand, letting a cigar burn away slowly in his fingers while making the odd comment to neighbouring players. Baccarat was the only game he indulged in and I dealt to him many times in my stay at the Sands. After hearing me speak and remarking on my accent he used to call me 'Scottie' and seemed to prefer my table to any other. During slack periods he would ask about Scotland. Where did I come from? Glasgow? Were there any Eyetalians there? He seemed amazed that they all had fish and chip and ice-cream shops and I didn't think it worth the bother of going into the VC pie interlude. Did I know any Calabrese among the Eyetalians? His parents were Calabrese, he said, pronouncing it 'Calabrace'. I didn't know what he was talk-ing about, until I found out later that Calabria was the region in Italy where his parents were born.

I cannot recall him ever taking a puff at his ever-present cheroot. He would hold it loosely between the first and second fingers of his right hand, and do everything with it in that position—lift his glass, take a few from a pile of chips, turn a card, rake in the occasional winnings, but the cigar never seemed to move from its position. His glass never seemed to need topping up and I wondered if that too was simply a comforter. Win or lose, his manner was always the same, quiet and pleasant, and he never failed to leave a handsome tip for the dealer. It was at that time that his son, a pilot in the US airforce, was killed in an air crash, and after that tragedy he never appeared at my baccarat table again. He would do his mandatory cabaret stint, then could be seen sit-ting alone and morose at the Sands bar, drinking heavily.

Sinatra too was a frequent visitor, but always appeared with two body-guards, one on either side, and would let one of them do the betting for him. He had no special preference; roulette, baccarat, craps, he spent some time at all the tables, and although I had been told that he was a heavy gambler I never saw any large bets being made on his behalf. I was left with the impression that his main purpose in visiting the Sands was to allow himself to be seen by admiring fans and he struck me as having a somewhat abrasive manner. He never spoke to any of the dealers and certainly didn't exude Dean Martin's warm and friendly aura.

Robert Redford was also to be seen often in the gaming room. His prefer-ence was for the roulette table, and he would write down each number as it came up, then consult a notebook, where, it was said, he had written down a system to beat the roulette wheel. He may have had a system with which to beat the house, but I was in charge of the wheel at his table once or twice, and I do not recollect him winning any more than any other average punter. He always wore dark glasses and was strictly a loner, oblivious to everyone around.

A very heavy gambler I remember dealing to on several occasions was an actor whose face I knew well from the countless B-pictures I had seen. His name was Albert Dekker, a big heavy-set man with one of those well-kent faces you see in many films. I remembered him as a gangster in a Burt Lancaster film, *The Killers*, and as a Pinkerton man in the William Holden western, *The Wild Bunch*. Always in the company of some glamorous blonde he spent hours at the baccarat tables and was a heavy punter, sometimes betting recklessly on indifferent cards. One morning, after a particularly heavy losing session at baccarat, he was found dead in his Los Angeles apartment under mysterious circumstances. He was dressed in women's underwear and appeared to have died from asphyxiation caused by a garter tied around his neck. His bizarre death caused a sensation in the press, and for days on end the tabloids reported the case with lurid headlines. Eventually the case fizzled out and the mystery of his death was never solved.

Lee Marvin, too, often made an appearance, and was no different in the flesh from the hard-bitten characters he played on film. His cigar and highball glass were definitely not just for show. He surrounded himself with clouds of tobacco smoke and kept asking for his glass to be refilled. He gambled hard. I once had to cover his $5000 bet on a baccarat hand, and his face showed not the slightest emotion when he went over the limit on his draw. He held his liquor well.

There was one little old man who appeared almost every day, sometimes to bet a few dollars on a blackjack hand before taking a seat in the bar where he would sip a soft drink and applaud the cabaret show. His face never changed expression. Buster Keaton was making the most of his old age.

While still a senator John F. Kennedy came frequently to see the Rat Pack cabaret at the Sands and mixed with them in the restaurant and bars, although he was never seen in the gaming rooms. His visits to the Sands stopped of course when he became president several years before my arrival there. He was a great fan of Sinatra's as he was of Dean Martin, and the two singers campaigned actively in his presidential campaign.

The Sands had without doubt the best entertainment in the whole of Vegas. Some of Sinatra's Rat Pack kept up the tradition they had established when they were making *Ocean's Eleven*, when they would film during the day and appear in the cabaret at night. They also did ad lib shows in the hotel when the fancy took them and when there were two or three of them present, which was often. Before the death of his son Dean Martin loved to play about and sing after a session at the tables; he and Sinatra were the perfect entertainers and did some marvellous impromptu acts together. I treasure the copy of an audio cassette of Dean Martin giving an impromptu solo performance on the cabaret floor, made by a casino electrician one night when the singer decided to give the customers some extra unrehearsed entertainment.

When I think back, it was a funny thing, but a large number of the entertainers who came to the Las Vegas casinos were 'Eyetalian'. There was Dean Martin himself, and Sinatra, Perry Como, Al Martino, Louis Prima and Tony Bennett, all of them of Italian extraction. One of the actors in *Ocean's Eleven* who was never to be seen in the Sands gaming rooms after the making of the film was Sammy Davies Jr. This was on account of the colour bar that still operated in the casinos then. If you were black you were allowed in to entertain the white customers with song and dance, but you were barred from gambling with them, drinking or eating with them or using the same toilets as the white folks did. Louis Armstrong blew his trumpet on several occasions at the Sands and at the Flamingo for the entertainment of the customers, but that was that. He loved to gamble, but after his performances he had to go to one of the 'Negro' joints at the back end of Glitter Gulch to throw the dice or turn a card.

The casinos vied one with the other in the entertainment they presented in their cabarets. The Sands had the exclusive use of the Frank Sinatra-Dean Martin crowd. Eddie Fisher appeared regularly at the Desert Inn. Ella Fitzgerald and Harry James were often to be heard singing and playing the trumpet respectively at the Flamingo. Louis Prima and his orchestra performed frequently at The Sahara, and the Sons of the Pioneers, singers of cowboy songs with their theme song 'Cool Water', were a permanent fixture there.

Frank Sinatra's long love affair with the Sands lasted until Howard Hughes bought the casino in 1967. On his instructions Sinatra's credit at the casino was cut off because, according to the new management, he was prone to forgetfulness about the money he owed them. The singer responded in a furious row with Carl Cohen, the new manager, in which he threw a chair at him and had one of his own teeth knocked out in the ensuing melee. Seeking revenge, the furious Sinatra sued the management for the cost of his dental repairs but was unsuccessful, since it was patently obvious that he had started the fracas. He then signed a contract with the rival Caesar's Palace, expecting his friends to follow him out of the Sands. But Dean Martin was very much his own man. He liked the ambience at the Sands, he had many friends there and instead of leaving negotiated a further year's contract with the management. At the end of that contract he moved to the nearby Riviera casino, where a ticket for a Dean Martin show cost more than one for Frank Sinatra's show at Caesar's Palace.

At the Sands I had to work two alternate shifts, one going from 2pm until 10pm and the other 10pm to 6am. This meant that the Sands, in common with most other casinos on the strip, closed for 6 hours in the 24, although by mutual arrangement the closing hours varied from casino to casino, so that 24-hour a day, 365-days-a year gambling was available on the strip. During the hours of closure an army of cleaners went to work sweeping and polishing the gaming rooms, bars and cabaret areas. Maintenance and resetting of the slot machines, if the latter was thought necessary, was also carried out. These machines could be adjusted to give the house any kind of odds the management cared to set, and it was considered good public relations occasionally to give the suckers who fed their money into them better odds than usual to encourage return visits. Not that any encouragement seemed to be necessary, for it appeared to me that a large percentage of the customers were addicted to playing the one-armed bandits. Many would spend the better part of the day wandering from machine to machine, paper cup in hand, putting in a dollar here and a dollar there until sheer exhaustion, both of money and of body, forced them to motel and bed. The next morning they would breakfast on junk food so as to add on a little more fat to their bodies and further clog up their arteries, join in a queue to cash in another social security cheque, and then back to the coin-filled paper cup and the ritual stance in front of the gaming machines with, in the case of the women, a work glove on the pulling hand.

My favourite shift was the 2 till 10. This had two advantages. Firstly it gave you a normal night's sleep, and since the afternoon session was never as busy as the night stint you did not have to operate under the same intense pressure as you were subjected to during the night. During the day the roulette croupier was allowed a 15-minute break every two hours, but during the night sessions the break came once every hour, and even with this you could come out of a night shift drained of all energy and with concentration near to breaking point. The other advantage of the afternoon session was that when working it I could find the time to relax on the golf course and get away from the frenetic atmosphere of downtown Las Vegas, for there is nowhere on the Strip or in the streets running off it where some silence and tranquillity can be found.

The noise from one casino blends into the noise from another. If it's not the constant background Muzak, it's the clatter of the one-armed bandits as they are played to the limit by the constant pull and noisy release of the lever. Background music pervades Las Vegas from the time you walk into the airport, and surrounds you everywhere you go. It is in the hotel reception area, in the corridors, in the swimming pool areas, in the bars, in the toilets and rest rooms, in the shops and drugstores, and leaks out into the broad pavements. There was nowhere you could relax with a drink without being subjected to featureless canned music of some sort, so I tried to get away from the downtown area as often as possible in search of peace and quiet.

The place I eventually found to get away from it all was a golf course recently constructed about 25 miles from Vegas along the shore of Lake Mead, the 115-mile-long artificial lake created by the construction of the Boulder Dam, although even here the clubhouse walls cooed some kind of music at you as you changed in and out of your golfing clothes. I spent as much of my free time on the course as I could, away from the brassy artificiality of the Las Vegas scene. I occasionally managed a game on the Desert Inn course, built at the rear of the Desert Inn complex, but the course was only a few hundred yards from the Strip and frequented by the hotel guests, so I preferred to drive the 25 miles or so to Lake Mead to get well away from the built-up downtown area.

One observation sums up the difference between Monte Carlo, once the Mecca of all gamblers, and Las Vegas the usurper. Las Vegas has become the American Monte Carlo, fifty times bigger of course, and without the elegance of its French precursor. To house the Monte Carlo casino the architect from Paris had designed a building whose elegant contours could have done service as an opera house, and whose interior could have graced any Royal Palace. For the grand opening, to which some of the crowned heads of Europe were invited, Sarah Bernhardt read a poem specially written for the occasion, and Caruso sang a selection of operatic arias. For the opening of the Flamingo, the first of the Vegas super-casinos, the architects chosen were the scene builders from the Hollywood studios. Among the artistes hired by Bugsy Siegel to entertain the guests were Abbot and Costello, together with the Three Stooges and Schnozzle Durante. Many of the guests were noted figures from the world of crime, in particular Myer Lansky, close friend and associate of the exiled Lucky Luciano. Sharing the same table were Vito Genovese, Carlo Gambino and Jack Dragna, the Mafia syndicate bosses.

One night at the Sands, while I was dealing baccarat at a quiet table, word began to spread through the room that Stu Ungar had just arrived at the casino. I had heard the name Stu Ungar mentioned often in conversation amongst dealers and gamblers, and although his fame had still to grow, I knew him as having acquired the reputation of being one of the sharpest card players ever to have set foot in Nevada. I couldn't help but feel a thrill of anticipation when he came into the gaming room and stopped at the table where I was dealing.

Stu Ungar, so went the story, was a school dropout who had become a professional gambler at 15, and at that age was already beating the best players in New York at his favourite game, gin rummy. Sep Young, a well-known New York bookie, saw Ungar at work in a gambling room in Harlem and was so impressed by the youth's performance that he put up the $500 stake money required to get him into a local high-stakes gin rummy tournament. Ungar won the $10,000 first prize without even losing a single hand, a record which stands in any gin rummy tournament to this day. He gave the bookie back the $500 plus $5000 of the winnings and kept the rest. He gave his father $1000 and then the very next day proceeded to lose the remaining $3500 on the horses at the Saratoga racetrack. That episode set the pattern of his gambling behaviour for the rest of his life; win at cards and lose it all fast at the races.

He then made his way down the coast to Miami, sitting in at any card game he could find, and winning something at all of them. In the Florida casinos he cleaned up at baccarat in a big way, winning thousands until all the houses conveniently declared the card tables closed as soon as he walked through the door. What he had won at the tables he soon had lost at the racetrack and so he arrived in Nevada without a cent to his name. A gambler who had seen him in action in New York—Benny Binion of the Horseshoe casino in Las Vegas—staked him into a $50,000 gin rummy tournament in a gambling joint in Reno. On the last hand, before showing his own winning combination and in a demonstration of his phenomenal memory, Ungar named every one of the losing player's cards!

He then came south to Las Vegas and began to apply his skills to blackjack, which in Caesar's Palace was played with a single deck shoe, as it was in most other Nevada casinos. In Caesar's Palace one night he won $83,000 in a run of play, and at that point the manager stopped the game. To show him how wise he had been Stu correctly identified the last remaining 18 cards in the shoe, and that was the end of single-deck blackjack in the casinos of Las Vegas. From then on four decks of cards were used in the game, which should have eliminated the possibility of memorising the cards.

When that happened, the story goes that Ungar offered to bet any takers $10,000 that he could name the last 15 cards in the four-deck shoe. Nobody took him up on that bet, so Ungar kept on upping the number of cards he would bet on to remember, until a punter named Stupak bet him ten to one—$100,000 to $10,000—that he couldn't name the last 25 cards in a four-deck game. Stu won the bet without hesitating a minute between calls, and stories of that feat are told to this day by the old-timers in Vegas. From then on Stupak staked him in poker tournaments and won a great deal of money by so doing, but Stu did as he had always done, winning huge sums, but losing it all the next day on the horses.

And there he was, standing in front of me!

Until then my game had not seen much action; two or three hundred dollars only had found its way into the house's pockets and I had two punters at the table betting no more than 10 or 20 dollars at a time. The news of Ungar's arrival had spread like wildfire throughout the casino, and by the time he had reached my table a crowd had gathered behind him to catch a glimpse of the great man at work. Usually, the Hollywood stars who frequent the Vegas casinos are the centre of attraction if they appear at any of the tables, but here the roles were reversed. In that crowd waiting to see Ungar in action were enough stars and bit players to make a Cecil B. De Mille movie. Stu Ungar slid onto a stool and the two impassive looking companions who had been with him since his entry took up a position on either side. Behind him stood another man, and I heard the name 'Stupak' mentioned by someone in the assembled crowd. Stupak reached into his pocket, pulled out a fat bankroll of $100 bills, peeled off ten of them and asked for a thousand dollar's worth of chips. I checked the bills, pushed out the chips to him and after he had checked the amount he passed them over to Ungar. I slid the notes through the cash slit into the box beneath. I then flexed and loosened my fingers, remembered my game with Kerry Packer at the Nassau Grand several years back and the $600,000 of the house's money I had lost to him, and wondered what kind of disaster Stu Ungar was going to dish out to me and to the house tonight.

Just as I was about to deal and start the game off I was stopped by a hand pulling on my arm from behind.

'Sorry gents, all card tables are now closing.'

I turned to see the casino manager, Louie Romano, standing behind me, accompanied as ever by his stone-faced bodyguard, smiling affably at the players.

'There's no problem, gents, no problem. Just a routine check of the shoes and the tables. The roulette tables are still open, the crap tables too, and you are all welcome to try your hand there.'

He smiled again, this time directly at Ungar and his companion.

'Pleasure to see you here, Stu, a great pleasure indeed, yes sir. Always glad to welcome a high roller like you here. It sure is an honour to have you with us, yes indeed. I sure wish you the best of luck at the wheel, there's a no-limit game there and that should suit you, Stu. There's the craps too, but I don't

74

believe that's your kind of game. In any case, the drinks are on the house for you and your three friends. It sure is a pleasure to have you here at the Sands.'

Romano kept on smiling through the hum of disappointment that rippled through the assembled onlookers. Ungar did not answer but looked at him with a face devoid of expression. Stupak grimaced and shrugged his shoulders and gathered the chips into his pocket. He exchanged glances with his companions and walked with them to the bar where they stood for half an hour or so sipping their free drinks. The chips were then cashed in and the four left without even a glance at the roulette tables. After his feat at Caesar's Palace no casino in Vegas would allow him to play in a card game, and after a while Ungar gave up trying, but continued to visit the casinos. The Sands was his favourite; the cabaret there was always first class, and he was always the loudest to applaud the act. He played and won occasionally at craps, a thousand dollars or so a game, but peanuts by his standards. He never once bet even a single dollar on a roulette wheel. No skill there, he'd say, just chance. No one ever asked him what the difference was in picking a number on a roulette wheel and picking the winner in a horse race.

With the card games at the casinos closed to him, Ungar entered his first World Poker Championship with Stupak as his sponsor and won it, and to show that it was no fluke he won it again the following year, pocketing nearly two million dollars for himself and his sponsor in the process. He quarrelled with Stupak over his cut of the winnings, took to drugs and drink and slowly disappeared from the big gambling scene, coming to the surface now and then to appear in small games in obscure clubs, winning just enough to feed his habits. Years later Stupak appeared once more on the scene and staked him the £10,000 entry to the World Poker Championship. His old skills came to the surface, and after four days of playing, the greatest comeback in gambling history had occurred. He won the million-dollar prize and set up a record for three wins in the championship, a feat equalled only by the legendary Western gambler, Johnny Moss.

Two months later he was broke again after losing his all on the horses, and was found dead in a cheap hotel room close by the racetrack after a drink and drugs session.

I often wonder how that baccarat game at my table at the Sands would have gone if he had been allowed to play. Louie Romano was later reported to have said that it might have been worth an $80,000 loss just to see him in action, but that the syndicate who owned the Sands at the time might not have seen it that way.

ELEVEN

THE HORSESHOE

My contract with the dealer's agency required me to work in any casino or gambling joint where they were asked to supply a dealer, and during my first year in Vegas I was moved around between four or five of the big casinos on the Strip. I did a spell in the Dunes, the Desert Inn, Caesar's Palace, and in the Silver Palace. All of them were much the same as each other apart from the décor; each had the same harsh multicoloured lighting and each was bathed with the same soothing electronic background Muzak. Each had a large area at the entrance furnished with row upon row of one-armed bandits, beyond which were the gaming rooms, bars, cabarets and restaurants. The players in each could well have been clones of the players in the previous casino.

The one exception as far as ambience was concerned was Caesar's Palace. The first of the 'theme park' Disneyland-type casinos, it resembled the set of a Hollywood Roman epic, a mixture of *Quo Vadis*, *Ben Hur*, *The Robe* and *The Sign of the Cross*. You almost expected to see Charlton Heston, Richard Burton and Frederick March sporting togas and decked out in centurion armour. The bar and cabaret waitresses were kitted out as Roman slaves, with a minimum of clothing to allow for plunging cleavages and provocative thighs, and with golden chains as ornaments to emphasise their station in life. The décor was dreamed up by some Hollywood set designer to present his own interpretation of what the interior of a Roman palace might have looked like, with soaring columns, marble floors and shallow bathing pools where scantily-clad maidens showed off their delights.

These vast hotel casinos all have one thing in common. They offer anyone with even a modest wallet a taste of the opulence and luxury and service that in other places are reserved for the very rich. None of these huge casinos attract the oil-rich Arabs and other big gamblers who frequent the famous London and European casinos and that is how the big Vegas casino owners want it. The men behind the scenes in Vegas are more interested in fast turnover than they are in the individual big-spending gambler and in turn the heavy gamblers find the rules in the Las Vegas casinos too restrictive. For example, if the heavy gamblers bet the table limit on a single number in roulette they are not allowed to double the bet on a split number, or treble or quadruple it on a three- or four-way chance, as they could in the European casinos. The big casinos also have a limit to the amount of money that can be bet on any one card. This limit—$500 as I remember it at the Sands— is the one adopted by all of the casinos on the strip, and this does not suit the big gamblers who like to feel that they are free to ride as high as they want on the crest of a winning streak.

The owners of the Strip casinos do not want million-dollar winners or million-dollar losers, although the welcome mat is laid out if they do appear. They want a bigger flow of more moderately betting customers to play at the tables, those who at most will win or lose in the tens or hundreds of thousands of dollars. If the occasional heavy gambler happens along, well and good, he is welcomed with open arms, representing as he does potential winnings to swell the house profits and make for good publicity; however, twenty gamblers each losing $5000 are of far greater value to the house than is the single gambler who loses $100,000. The greater the flow of customers, the more is spent on hotel rooms and the greater is the money pouring into the restaurants and bars, increasing the profit for the owners.

One morning I was instructed to report to the Horseshoe in Fremont Street, just off the main Strip, on the edge of an area known as Glitter Gulch. Glitter Gulch was patronised by hard gamblers and by the lower end of the tourist industry. Downtown Las Vegas, as this district was also known, was strictly for gambling, there was nothing else to do and nowhere else to go except for the dozens of seedy gambling joints to be found along Fremont Street, Glitter Gulch's main thoroughfare. Sandwiched in between the many gambling joints were dozens of dingy shops peddling cheap western-style clothes and gaudy souvenirs. There were scores of girlie bars where dancers, naked except for a few wisps of see-through nylon, gyrated sensuously to thumping music, their long-past sell-by date masked by the dim strobe lighting. Busloads of daytrippers were ferried into this area from the Los Angeles district. Most were pensioners, the women in their garish lime- or banana-coloured yellow shorts encasing huge bottoms and exposing sagging thighs and wrinkled knees. The men, who for some reason appeared to be quite thin in comparison to their spouses, trailed behind them decked out in their sky-blue jackets, overlong Bermuda shorts, baseball caps and ill-fitting plastic teeth.

These day trippers stayed in small run-down motels with basic amenities and with no swimming pools. Not for them the luxury casinos on the adjacent Strip, although some did venture into the slot-machine areas of the big gaming houses. They flocked in their thousands into the seedy casinos of Fremont Street, the women with a cupful of small change in one hand and a glove on the other to pull on the levers of the machines while the men shot craps for a dollar, played fifty-cent-a-time blackjack and drew cards for two-dollar-limit stud poker. Some were physical wrecks in wheelchairs and seemed to be afflicted by every ailment known to man. Some were mobile and shuffled along arthritically with the help of walking sticks, but all would have cashed in their social security cheques and disability allowances in the vain hope of winning a miracle jackpot. It was a sad spectacle to see and stripped their old age of all dignity.

The Horseshoe, situated at the respectable end of Fremont Street, where it joins the Strip, belonged to Benny Binion, who has become a legend amongst the gambling fraternity in the same way that John Wayne is a legend in the making of Western films. Men and cities and countries can be judged by the heroes they venerate, and the fact that there are only two historic equestrian statues in the city of Las Vegas tells you all about Vegas and its values. There is a statue erected to the memory of Rafael Rivera, said to be the first white man to find the Las Vegas valley, and then there is the statue of Benny Binion, said to be the first gambling house owner in Las Vegas to give gamblers a fair deal and a shot at winning big money with his no-limit betting policy. The Binion statue, by the same sculptor who fashioned the John Wayne statue that stands at the portals of Los Angeles airport, makes the statement that Las Vegas puts on a pedestal the Western traditions of individuality, straight-shooting and a good and fair gamble.

In affirmation of this, the entrance to Benny Binion's Horseshoe casino consisted, as it still does, of a seven-foot-high horseshoe with its edges painted in gold. Set in the middle, blending in with the arch of the horseshoe, there is a glass-fronted ornate wooden frame. In this frame were one hundred ten thousand dollar bills, adding up to a total of one million dollars. Standing guard over this fortune there was a tough-looking guard in cowboy costume complete with Stetson and a pair of low-slung Colt 45s. His presence there was purely for show, I suspect, for a sheet of bullet-proof glass protects this extravagant display of cash and the risk of theft is low, since $10,000 bills are no longer in circulation, and a thief would find it impossible to have them changed outside of a federal bank.

Benny Binion was born in 1904 on a horse ranch in Texas, and as a boy he accompanied his father around the West on his journeys as a horse trader. He became skilled as a horse dealer and had his first taste of gambling in the camps around the cow towns of Arizona, Texas and New Mexico, where traders gathered to await market days. He soon became wise to the methods used by the players to give themselves a cheating advantage in the card games. A quick learner, he was not long in noticing that crooked gamblers had their own individual way of marking critical cards: some left a tiny scrape on the card with a fingernail, some gave a small, almost imperceptible twist to the corner of a card, any mark that would give them an advantage in a game. These were dangerous procedures, which, if detected, could often give rise to sudden deadly gun fights, and the young Binion was no stranger to the sight of a dead man being hastily dragged out of the room after a shoot-out at a card table. Cheating was not confined to card games. There were some who would try to cheat at dice, a favourite method being the placing of a small speck of adhesive material on a die, which would result in it slowing up and stopping with the chosen number up. The young Binion soon became expert in picking out the crooked ones amongst the gamblers, and in later years would boast that all he had to do to determine the honesty of a player was to watch him play one hand at poker or make one throw of the dice.

In 1920, at sixteen years of age, Binion left the family horse ranch and made his way to Dallas to seek his fortune. At first the boy ran errands for professional gamblers, steering would-be card players to clandestine gambling joints where the professionals would skilfully deprive them of their cash. When Prohibition became part of the law of the land in the early twenties, he diversified and began to make money by smuggling bootleg liquor from Mexico across the Rio Grande into Texas. His bootlegging activities led him to kill a man in Dallas in 1931 and to be charged with murder. Binion suspected fellow bootlegger Frank Bolding of having stolen some bottles of illicit whisky from his cache and confronted him with his suspicions. The argument soon turned to violence, and although Bolding was an expert in knife-fighting with more than one kill to his name, Binion beat him to the draw with a six-gun, shot him in the neck and killed him. Binion claimed that he had killed in self-defence, was given the benefit of the doubt by the judge and was handed a two-year suspended sentence. Since Bolding had many friends in Dallas who were certain to seek revenge, Binion reckoned that it would now be too dangerous to stay, so he moved over the Nevada state line to Las Vegas, at that time a small dusty railway town catering mainly for miners, gold prospectors, cowboys and soldiers on leave from the neighbouring Fort Baker.

Even in the Depression years of the thirties, Nevada and its neighbour Texas were awash with money created by the huge cattle ranches and the rapidly developing oil industry of the region. With the outbreak of World War Two Binion came into his own and hit the big time. With the money made from his bootlegging activities he bought over the Horseshoe, a seedy little gambling joint at the corner of Fremont Street and the main Las Vegas strip, renovated it with velvet drapes to cover the timber walls and carpets to cover the rough wooden floors. He gave it the final touch with crystal chandeliers suspended from wagon wheels hung onto the ceiling. It retained its Western atmosphere, and as Binion's reputation for honest no-limit gambling spread it attracted serious gamblers, and soon became one of the busiest casinos in Vegas. Its reputation came at a price, however. The flow of money to be seen there attracted all sorts of desperate characters to Binion's Horseshoe. In those days Binion carried three pistols: two .45 automatics and a small .38 revolver, and one night he got into a gun fight with a rival numbers operator, Ben Frieden, and shot him dead. Binion himself was wounded and again was cleared on grounds of self-defence.

Binion made the Horseshoe famous throughout the gambling world of the American West as being the only casino where a no-limit rule applied as long as the player made it on his first bet. He set the craps limit at $500, ten times the maximum at any other casino. Most serious gamblers use some sort of system to work the tables. Typically, if a gambler wins a ten-dollar bet at craps, he will then bet the original ten dollars plus the ten dollars won. All gamblers dream of riding a streak of luck into really big money at craps in this way, but a house limit made it much harder to do so on the one run of dice. A player betting ten dollars and doubling it each time he won would be blocked on the fourth bet by the fifty-dollar limit set by other casinos. Under Binion's $500 limit, he could keep doubling an original ten-dollar stake until the seventh bet. If the gambler won all seven bets he could win $1130 at Binion's compared to $270 anywhere else. The new limits made the Horseshoe famous immediately, and serious gamblers would not go anywhere else to play.

Binion's fame had spread to the extent that he himself had become a tourist attraction and people came not only to gamble at the Horseshoe but to see and speak to the living legend in person. He and his sons changed poker from a kitchen-table back-room pastime into an important casino game. The big casinos did not offer poker because it was not entirely respectable, more a card game of bluff rather than of skill which attracted many shady characters, but Binion set aside special poker rooms to let at $2000 per 5-hour session, including the services of an honest and impartial house dealer. He was the promoter who made Las Vegas the home of the World Championship Poker Finals Rodeo, as it was advertised, played out at the Horseshoe every December.

The original world championship games were winner-take-all challenges open to anybody with $10,000 to buy in. This open aspect of the tournament was the secret of its fame and success; it lured rich suckers and unknown poker-playing hopefuls, but it also lured legendary pros such as Stu Ungar and others, who hoped to deprive the newcomers of their cash. This they usually did, given their skill and expertise, but sometimes the unknowns won and themselves became legends, and that hope spurred newcomers on to return time and time again.

Binion's devised special rules to force the poker games to a resolution before everyone got bored with the length of the games, some of which could last for many hours, and they made it into a nationally televised event. The television coverage given to the poker championships brushed off the lingering air of disrepute attached to the game, so that eventually nearly every other casino in Vegas added the game of poker to the attractions of the house, with special rooms set aside for players. To this day the Horseshoe continues to host the World Championship of Poker. Benny himself is long dead, but his family carries on the event, which now attracts poker players from all over the world.

When I first appeared at the Horseshoe I felt as if I had been transported onto the set of a movie I had seen years ago in Glasgow. The film was called *Big Deal at Dodge City*, and starred Henry Fonda as a gambler who pretends to be a gullible farmer who connives, with the help of his wife and a local small-town banker, to cheat a roomful of poker players out of a great deal of money. In the film his headquarters as a gambler are in a lavishly appointed casino in an unnamed Western town. I was later to learn that Binion's Horseshoe had been recreated in a Hollywood set for the purposes of the film.

The Horseshoe was comparatively small, and could have fitted into a corner of any of the big casinos on the Strip. Once through the entrance and past the framed million dollars at the door you entered a small ante-room containing about thirty or so one-armed bandits, all programmed to take ten-dollar tokens. There were six or so hard-eyed boxmen patrolling the room. No fat–bottomed, fifty-cents-a-time, daytripper tourist trade here. At ten dollars a time these machines were talking about serious money, and the characters playing them did not linger. Twenty tokens or so were enough to speculate on the chance of winning a $25,000 jackpot, which consisted of twenty-five $1000 tokens which could be changed into cash at the cashier's cage. Winking neon letters along one wall spelled out the fact that no casino employee was allowed to play at the machines, a reference to the rumour that in some casinos the jackpots were won only by the house itself.

I presented myself to the floor manager at nine in the morning and even at that early hour the place was full of people. In the gaming room there were two roulette tables, surrounded by men in cowboy boots and Stetson hats For some reason or other that I could never figure out, men wearing Stetson hats didn't seem to want to remove them. The six card tables and the two crap games were similarly busy, with players perched in semi circles around the baccarat tables and even the seats in a little adjoining Keno lounge were mostly taken. At one corner of the main gambling floor a narrow passage led to four private rooms set aside for poker or any other card game the hirer of the room cared to play, and at the other a stairway led down to a restaurant decorated out as a traditional Western saloon. The menu there consisted of either huge T bone steaks or roast chicken with a veg on the side served on huge metal plates by waiters, most of them Mexican in vaquero costume. In the gaming room there was no hint of Disneyland glitter. No all pervading Musak, just the droning commands of the croupier, heard against the background sound of chips being placed on the table, followed by the clicking of the ivory ball as it came to rest on someone's lucky number.

Heavy cigarette and tobacco smoke floated in the air, with the conditioning unit just efficient enough to keep the atmosphere breathable. There were no casino based hookers around that I could see, and by now I was an expert in the spotting of them. Each of the big hotel casinos, without exception, tolerated, if not actually encouraged, the presence of high class expensively dressed hookers at the gaming tables as an added attraction for the customer to sample if he so wished. This is how the process functioned. A couple of attractive hookers would work the roulette tables, making occasional small bets whilst eyeing up prospective clients. When a contact was made, the twosome would go up to reception and ask for a private room for the night, the hooker having made it clear that if the customer already had a room at the hotel she would not perform there, since it might lead to complications with any possible wife or existing companion, not to mention the possibility of a gang-bang, a not unheard-of occupational hazard. No amount of pleading by the customer would make them bend this rule, there always would be another client if this one withdrew. The room would be let to the customer for the night at top prices and the business done. An hour later the hooker would be back at another table looking for another client and the procedure would be repeated several times in the one night. The hotel made a profit in three ways. Firstly, the hookers were all top class material and made the place look good, secondly, the hotel could let out at top prices several times each day rooms which would otherwise be empty, and thirdly many of the hookers were themselves hooked on gambling and would lose a good percentage of their night's earnings to the house. But that was not for Binion's. The house ran a strict policy: no unaccompanied females allowed.

Informality was the keynote in the gaming rooms there. Benny Binion, who by the time of my arrival had relinquished the management of the Horseshoe to his family, moved around the floor dressed in a traditional Western outfit with gold coins for buttons on his cowboy shirts, stopping for a word here and there with a friend or acquaintance and making a point of exchanging pleasantries with the dealers and boxmen. By now well into his seventies, he was a huge man well over six feet in height, with a pleasant smiling face which belied all the stories I had heard told about him. He had been forced to give up control of the Horseshoe to his sons, for in the 1950s Benny had served a one-year prison sentence for tax evasion, stemming not from the casino profits but from his Texas operations, and since a convicted felon could not hold a gaming licence in Nevada, his sons took over the running of the casino. The informality of the Horseshoe was also reflected in the uniform of the dealers and croupiers. At all the other casinos I had dealt in the dealers were dressed in formal suits with white shirt and bow tie. Here we wore white smartly-cut cowboy shirts and a narrow black western-style bow tie with two long tails on which the word 'Horseshoe' was inscribed. The white shirts marked us out as dealers; the boxmen and pit bosses wore similar shirts in black. As in all other casinos, the no-pocket rule applied. In all other respects there was no difference from other gambling rooms: the blackjack players perched on their high stools waiting for the card that would beat the dealer; the crap-shooters eagerly circling the crap tables, urging the dice to fall as they wanted them to, and everywhere the boxmen, who watched the pit bosses, who watched the dealers, who in turn watched the players, who watched the fall of the cards, the spin of the wheel and the bounce of the dice.

My first station at the Horseshoe was at one of the roulette tables, where I was impressed by the size of the bets being placed, some of them ten times greater than I had been accustomed to in the Strip casinos. The betting chips were distinctive. Different colours had different values, as in all casinos, but here there was a difference. All chips were decorated with the casino's horseshoe symbol, and set in the middle of the symbol was a picture of a smiling Benny Binion in a cowboy hat. I had also to learn that the serious gamblers in the Horseshoe always leave out the zeros when a bet is announced. In their parlance a nickel is $500, a dime is $1000 and a big dime is $10,000, so until I became accustomed I had to concentrate on the chips being placed and not on the words being uttered. The clients at the table were all serious gamblers. No shrieks of joy and clapping of hands from a female winner (there were a few escorted females present), no bursts of laughter or shouts from slightly tipsy punters, no animated conversation on the part of the onlookers. Just the sound of gamblers and dealers going about their business, set against a low hum of conversation from the drinkers at the liquor bar.

I was moved from station to station and took a turn at blackjack and craps, where again I was amazed at the size of the bets being placed: $5000 lost on a single throw of the dice; $10,000 bet and lost on a single card at blackjack; $25,000 lost on a number at roulette. Such losses sustained without as much as a quiver of a face muscle. Small wonder that the Horseshoe was reputed to be the most profitable casino in the whole of Vegas. True to its Western tradition, the Horseshoe was the only casino where I saw the dice game chuck-a luck played. This is played with three dice in a wire cage or cone-shaped horn, made of leather or metal. The name 'tinhorn gambler' derives from those gamblers who set up games of chuck-a-luck with low stakes and a horn fashioned out of tin cans, which was far cheaper than a leather one. The horn contains a series of inclined planes that tumble the dice as they fall out.

I once dealt at two private poker sessions of seven players, at one of which I saw the legendary Amarillo Slim Preston in action. This game started at 9.30 in the morning in one of the private rooms. The men chatted amongst themselves amicably whilst unloading their racks of chips and arranging them at their place at the table. There were massed towers of $100 black chips, piles of grey $500 chips and a few stacks of green $25 ones. Some of the players pulled out wads of banknotes from their pockets, fresh from the bank, and held together with paper bands on which was printed '5000 Dollars'. There must have been half a million dollars or so piled on that table, and this at 9.30 in the morning! Each of these poker sessions lasted the best part of six hours. The degree of concentration required of a dealer at such prolonged games makes a rest period of fifteen minutes or so every two hours necessary when he is substituted by a relief dealer, but even with these breaks I was tired at the end of the session. I calculated that more than a million dollars changed hands at that particular game.

Amarillo Slim had won the World Poker Championsip the year before, in 1970. He had then had made a name for himself as a commentator on TV and had appeared in a movie called *California Split* with Elliot Gould and George Segal. In the film the two stars played a couple of wandering gamblers doing the rounds of gambling joints in California, with Amarillo Slim in the role of a card sharp who takes them both to the cleaners. He had also been employed as the adviser for the gambling scenes in the popular 1960s TV series, *Maverick*, starring a young James Garner.

Amarillo Slim had a favourite saying: 'Poker is a game of people, it's not the hand I hold that matters, it's the people I play with.'

He was once interviewed on television and asked if he had ever been beaten in a poker game with strangers. His answer to the female interviewer was: 'Well, I'll tell you, Susie, very seldom do the lambs slaughter the butcher.'

He was nothing if not ostentatious, wearing high leather cowboy boots with spades, diamonds, hearts and clubs engraved on them, encircled with his name. He too wore golden coins for buttons on his Western shirt, his cuff-links were made out of $5 gold pieces, and his gold-coloured Cadillac sported two gold-tipped bull horns set into the radiator. He was also a man of strict principles as regards personal behaviour, and refused to be quoted in a book being written about his poker rival Stu Ungar.

'He's a wasted talent,' was his remark. 'I'm real square about drugs and don't make no bones about it. I tolerated Stu at the poker table, but I hate what he stood for.'

Perhaps the fact that Stu Ungar had beaten him one year in the finals of the Poker Championships had something to do with his dislike for the man.

My stint at the Horseshoe lasted for four months and was the one I enjoyed most in my two-year stay in Las Vegas. It had all the essence of the American West, with a vibrancy and a character about it that I was never to experience in any other casino. After that I did some work in the Las Vegas Grand as a croupier, then in the Silver Palace as a croupier and faro dealer.

The Silver Palace was one of the few casinos where faro was still played, and I had to go through a learning process to deal at that game. Although it was out of favour in almost all of the big casinos, a few of the smaller ones still provided faro as a nostalgic attraction for their customers. Faro was a card game introduced into New Orleans by the French in the early years of the nineteenth century, with the cards used having a picture of an Egyptian pharoah on the back, hence the name faro. The game is far more complicated than either baccarat or blackjack, involves all kinds of winning permutations, and because of the slowness of play is not suited to the fast turnover required by modern gambling houses. In view of its complexity I reckon it to be the most stressful of the card games to deal at and to control.

I was then given two weeks in a dive in Glitter Gulch known as Goodman's Nite Spot, where I had to work as a keno operator, a line of work that hardly requires a high degree of brain power. Keno as played in Nevada is merely a glorified form of the Bingo which is so popular amongst the old age pensioners in Glasgow, the only difference being that in Goodman's Nite Spot the players yelled out their winning numbers with an American accent, ate hamburgers instead of fish suppers and drank beer instead of Irn Bru. I complained about that posting in no uncertain terms and I was transferred back to the Sands for the remainder of my Las Vegas contract.

TWELVE

THE GAMBLERS' BOOKSHOP

Ever since my old foreman John McCluskey had introduced me to the Mitchell Library in Glasgow (a time that now seemed like a century ago), I had become a chain book reader, and always had something lying around that I could read during my rest breaks in the casinos. In Las Vegas I searched the length and breadth of the town for a library or bookshop where I could find something of interest. Las Vegas was hardly a centre of literary excellence, and I did not expect to find a Waterstones or some such concern, but I did think that somewhere among the hundreds of gambling dens, bars and strip joints that lined the side streets there would be some kind of bookshop with something worthwhile to read on its shelves. However, I could find nothing other than the dingy porno magazine and lurid paperback sellers which lined the sleazy streets of Glitter Gulch. It was hard enough to find a place to buy a newspaper, even, let alone a book.

Finally I was directed to a bookshop which could have found a market only in a town like Vegas, a low, rambling building with a triangular sign which read: The Gamblers' Bookshop.

Situated in Charleston Boulevard and opened in 1964, the shop is probably the only one of its kind in the world. It was opened in that year by Jack and Jenny Luckman, a husband and wife croupier team who had worked a lifetime in gambling houses the length and breadth of the United States. Now in their fifties, by the 1960s they had reached the end of their useful life as dealers. The working life of a dealer is not a very long one, especially at the roulette table, where you have to have razor-sharp mental and physical reflexes and a deep reservoir of stamina to deal with the pressures of running a busy table. While the card tables are not so physically demanding, you would be hard put to find a middle-aged croupier in charge of a roulette table at any casino.

Usually, having reached that stage, the croupier takes a step up the ladder and becomes a boxman or pit boss, but to fill these positions you must be possessed of a character with a hard and ruthless streak to deal firmly and decisively with the problems that crop up regularly in the gaming rooms; the slack dealer at a blackjack or baccarat table who inadvertently or otherwise allows his cards to be seen when dealing, or the downright dishonest one who deals to an accomplice from a stacked deck; the roulette croupier who is suspected of favouring certain of his clients in the determination of where exactly a bet has been placed, whether on a number, on a line or on a crossed line; the craps dealer who is not as particular as he should be in examining a set of dice which suddenly develop an uncommon winning streak, all these have to be ruthlessly dealt with by the pit boss or boxman and the offender got rid of on the spot. The pit boss must also be ready to deal with the odd angry client who finds himself on a losing streak and becomes dangerously aggressive, although in such situations an army of bouncers is always on hand to help. All in all, to be a boxman or a pit boss you cannot be a nice person, and Jack and Jenny Luckman were just that, two nice people who had come to the end of their usefulness as croupiers and dealers and had no desire to climb higher up the ladder in the gambling hierarchy.

They loved gambling and the gambling scene, however, and since there was nothing they did not know about the profession to which they had devoted their lives, they hit upon the idea of opening up a bookshop dealing exclusively with books on gambling for dealers and gamblers. Under the pen name of Walter I. Nolan (WIN), they wrote a series of little books called 'The Facts of…': Blackjack; Roulette; Craps; Keno; Baccarat; and Poker, which were an immediate success among the gambling fraternity and sold hundreds of copies. They could hardly print these booklets fast enough, and from their small original shop they started a mail order business. Through this thay circulated the books to every corner of the US and sales rose into the thousands.

Their shop very quickly became a meeting place for some of the most colourful characters in Las Vegas. There was not a single casino owner, dealer, manager, poker player, blackjack and baccarat theorist, faro dealer or craps shooter who from time to time did not frequent the place and spend hours there discussing the finer points of their favourite game. You would also be sure of finding some Hollywood scriptwriter or director there, looking for authentic material for a film, plus casting directors in search of some real-life hard-faced types to give an aura of realism to a gambling scene. I was fascinated by the books on the shelves: on the strategy of poker, the calculation of odds, procedures in baccarat and blackjack, biographies of famous gamblers, detailed accounts of famous poker encounters, books on the relative merits of the various makes of roulette tables and casino equipment, lists of every casino and gambling house in the USA and Mexico, everything in fact that might be of interest to anyone in the gambling profession.

Half a dozen or so drinkers were lounging at a bar at one end of the shop, smoking and drinking and talking animatedly to some others seated at one of the six or so tables there. One of the figures there had a familiar look. Amarillo Slim Preston looked up as I entered, smiled broadly and beckoned me over. Was I not the dealer at the poker game at the Horseshoe the day before? I was. With an accent like that I had to be from Scotland? I agreed. He waved his friends over for an introduction. They had names that could have come straight out of a Damon Runyon story: Johnny Moss, Dave Skiansky, Bob Stupak, Fast Eddie Seremba and an improbable character by the name of Fats Yocum (at least that's what it sounded like). They all gave me a warm welcome and seemed happy just to hear me speak in what they called my funny accent. Amarillo Slim had always wanted to visit Scotland, he said, to see the all the great golf courses there. St Andrews he just had to see some day, he had heard all about the famous Road Hole and wanted to see for himself if that bunker was as fearsome as everyone said it was and if the road was as difficult to play from as he had been told. Had I ever played St Andrews? He seemed disappointed when I had to answer in the negative. Did I know the Troon course? That postage-stamp short hole, just a hundred and twenty yards long, that must be quite some hole, some guys went into double figures there, so he had been told. Amarillo Slim knew more about the courses of Scotland than I did. He kept on at length about golf. It was his sport and relaxation, he said. He had helped design the Desert Inn course, and his friend and occasional golfing partner Jack Nicklaus had asked him to come and give an opinion on a course he was he was laying out at Lake Tahoe. Did I play golf?

I thought of the golf clubs my father and mother had quarrelled about many years ago, and the balls I used to pinch at the first hole at Ruchill, then of the games I had played in the Bahamas. Yes, I did. Great, he said. Where did you play back in Scotland? My mind raced to think of a course I knew something about. One came to mind that Rose and I used to walk across down on the Ayrshire coast. Prestwick, I answered. Great course, he replied. Marvellous hazard there, they call it the cardinal bunker. There's a hole called 'the Himalayas'. Did I know it? How would I like to make up a foursome next day at the Desert Inn?

I must have turned pale at the thought of the $1000 dollar bets he had been nonchalantly making at the poker table the day before, for he seemed to read my thoughts, and laughed. We play a twenty dollar Nassau, he explained. Five bucks on the first nine holes, five on the second nine and ten bucks on the match. Most you can win or lose is twenty bucks. How's about that?

And so early the next morning I was on the first tee at the Desert Inn course partnered by Fast Eddie Seremba against Amarillo Slim and Bob Stupak. The name Stupak had sounded familiar, and during the night it had come back to me. He was the one who had accompanied Stu Ungar at the Sands the night Louie Romano had closed the baccarat tables. Not a glimmer of recognition had crossed his face when introduced to me; he had been at the table only for a few minutes before Romano had called off, so he probably had taken no notice of the dealer. In point of fact very few gamblers ever take notice of the dealer, we are all faceless men with a pair of hands to deal a card or spin a wheel as far as most punters are concerned.

A good ten minutes were taken up on the first tee at the Desert Inn in an argument about handicaps. They accepted my 16 without demur, but I thought it strange that players who obviously played together as often as they did should have to argue about how many strokes they should give one another, until I realised that the arguments were all part of a ritual these friends indulged in before a game. Once started the game was played in deadly seriousness. Short putts were meticulously studied, controversial lies discussed at length, every rule meticulously adhered to and a book of regulations was always on hand to be consulted in the event of a problem. The game lasted the best part of four and half hours, which from their comments seemed fast play to them, but deadly slow to me. At the end of it Eddie Seremba and I had won the full Nassau, twenty dollars each, from which of course we had to pay for the drinks at the nineteenth hole.

Despite what to me seemed to be slow and over-meticulous play, I enjoyed the game thoroughly. The day was fine, the course was beautifully laid out and isolated from the ugly urban sprawl around it and the company I was in, interesting, to say the least. They must have enjoyed playing with me too, for another game was arranged for another day that week. In the meantime I asked quietly around about my partner Fast Eddie Seremba, and was amazed to find that this quiet little man, as he was on the golf course, was the best crap player ever to have played the Vegas casinos. He always played at great speed, hence the nickname and was reputed never to have left a crap table as a loser.

For the next game we tossed for partners and I drew Bob Stupak as my partner for the day. Again there was the pre-game argument about strokes. I was hailed as a bandit for claiming 16 as a handicap and was docked two strokes, much to the disgust of my new partner, who now had a diminished chance of getting his money back. For this game we were joined by a spectator, a friend of the three gamblers whose golfing days now lay behind him and who occasionally joined up with them for the company. Even I, a newcomer to the Las

Vegas scene, had heard of the great Johnny Moss. I had heard him spoken about in my Glasgow Chevalier days as perhaps the best poker player in the history of gambling. Together with Benny Binion, Moss was largely responsible for the development of high-stakes poker in Las Vegas during the glory days of Binion's Horseshoe Club, when the Fremont Street casino was the undisputed centre of the poker scene. Moss had become a fixture at the Horseshoe. He played countless games of poker in the casino's private rooms, and he won three World Series of Poker championships there, a feat matched only by Stu Ungar. This is an even more astounding accomplishment since the tournament didn't exist until late in his life. Johnny Moss, quite simply, was 'The Man' in professional poker—and was acknowledged to be so even among the flamboyant types who gather around the poker tables.

Like Benny Binion, Moss grew up the hard way in the early 1920s in Texas. He played his first game of cards at the age of 10, and lived and played with a bunch of low-life cheats and grifters who taught him all the con tricks of the trade, such as dealing from the bottom of the pack, hiding extra cards up your sleeve and how to mark a card with a fingernail. As a teenager he had become so adept at flushing out cardsharps that, at high stakes poker games run in local saloons, he would be given the job of keeping watch on the game to make sure there were no cheats amongst the players. At these games Moss learned all there was to be known about poker strategy and how to interpret the facial expressions and body language of a player so as to determine whether he was bluffing or not. Like most professional gamblers back in those early days, Moss soon took to the road and played in poker games wherever he could find them, rather than wait in the one gambling joint and wait for the games to come to him. He always played an honest game, although his cheating skills could have taken in all but the very best players. His skill was such that he could make enough money playing the game straight, so that cheating at cards seemed like more trouble than it was worth, which indeed it was, since cheating could earn you a bullet in the chest or at best a sound beating. His knowledge of how to cheat was a valuable asset, however, and he could tell whether a game was crooked or not as soon as a few hands had been played. These games could sometimes lead to trouble, so Moss usually carried a gun, and, like Binion, was not a man you messed around with.

During a TV interview in his later years he was asked if he had ever killed a man. His response was that he had shot plenty, but couldn't say if any of them had died! Moss finally settled down at the Horseshoe and lived for several years in the bungalow at the back of the Flamingo where Bugsy Siegel had been murdered. His reputation as a good and honest gambler attracted players from every part of the USA who queued up to test their skill against him. He had a lengthy and mutually beneficial relationship with the Horseshoe and Benny Binion, who would often provide financial backing for him in games where the stakes were too high for Moss alone to stump up. The story is told, true or not, that in what might have been the biggest single poker win in history, Moss, backed by Binion, bled the legendary gambler Nick 'the Greek' Dandalos out of a reported $2 million dollars. This happened in 1949, when Nick the Greek asked Binion to arrange a no-limit poker marathon between him and Moss. Binion agreed with the stipulation that the game be played in public view. The game lasted for four weeks, and Dandalos, who was a rich man in his own right and did not need the services of a backer, finally withdrew, having impoverished himself to the tune of $2 million.

Johnny Moss was very knowledgeable about golf and preferred to talk about golf and golfers rather than his own exploits in the field of gambling. In his later years he had taken to playing on the many courses that were springing up in the Las Vegas area, and played from an 18 handicap, which was not at all bad for a man who had taken up the game in his early sixties. His favourite course was the Sahara, the course built by the owners of the hotel casino of the same name and which each year hosted a tournament, the Sahara Invitational, attended by all the great American professionals of the sixties and seventies. In the pro-ams which always preceded these tournaments he boasted of having partnered Arnold Palmer, Jack Nicklaus and Julius Boros in successive years and of having won with them each year. He spoke proudly of having met all of the British Ryder Cup team in 1963. In that year the Ryder Cup match had been played on a course in Atlanta in Georgia and it was arranged that afterwards the entire British team should be flown to Las Vegas to participate in the Sahara tournament as guests of the Sahara Hotel.

Moss accompanied us round the course on our buggy and plied me with questions about golf in Scotland, much to the disgust of Bob Stupak, who complained afterwards that Moss's constant chatter had put him off his game and had caused us to lose ten dollars in the Nassau.

The Gamblers' Bookshop became a favourite haunt of mine, and I went there as often as I could. The place was always full of colourful characters, and they all gave a warm welcome to the little dealer from Scotland. 'Little', I suppose, I was by comparison, for although I was of average height, about 5' 8" or so, Amarillo Slim and his companions were all well over six feet in height and I felt dwarfed in their company. I enjoyed listening to them talk shop; they discussed card games in the same way that a golfer will analyse a game of golf, and from them I got a great insight into the mind of the professional gambler.

Almost without exception they all stayed away from games of pure chance. Roulette is for the suckers, they would say; card games have an element of chance in the cards you are dealt, but then your own ability to work with the cards you get comes into play and the game lies in outplaying your opponent with them. Fast Eddie Seremba claimed that as far as he was concerned craps was a game of skill and that technique played a large part in throwing the dice, and despite his companions' scepticism his record of winnings spoke for itself. The truth is that, as is the case in all sports, in gambling a good professional will always beat a good amateur, and that is how the professional gambler makes his living, by winning money from rich amateur gamblers who are addicted to the gaming table and are willing to match their inferior skills against his.

I played several rounds of golf with Fast Eddie Seremba and during the course of these games I learned more from him about dice and craps than I could ever have picked up in a lifetime's reading. Did I know, he asked, that dice were the oldest gambling instruments known to man? Dice identical in shape and size to the ones in use today had been found in Egyptian tombs dating back to 3000 BC, he said. Did I know that the ancient Chinese had dice? Dice had been found in Chinese excavations dating back to thousands of years BC. Did I know that the Greeks and Romans played games of dice similar to the ones we played today? They cast their dice from cup-shaped containers and played different types of games requiring the simultaneous use of two, three, four or even five sets of dice in games similar to our chuck-a-luck and poker dice. Did I know that a skilled dice thrower could make dice skid and slide so that the top face when it comes to rest will be the same as when it left his hand? That was the reason why in craps the dice had to be bounced against the far wall of the table. Did I know that in private games a cheat, if he were willing to run the risk of discovery, could often successfully introduce a pair of dice perfect in every respect apart from the elimination or addition of one dot on one of the six sides, thereby making the throwing of some numbers impossible? This scam was much more prevalent than you would think, he said. A suspicious examiner looks for loaded dice and 99% of the time doesn't notice the addition or the removal of a dot. Fast Eddie was a walking encyclopedia on the subject of dice and made me look at the game with a much broader understanding.

Of all the gamblers who frequented the bookshop, Amarillo Slim was perhaps the most knowledgeable about the history of poker as it had developed in the US. French soldiers brought a game called 'poque' to New Orleans around 1820, he told me, when it was played with a 20-card deck. After a shuffle, five-card hands were dealt face down to four players, who proceeded to bet on the relative strength of their cards. But even if you did not have a good hand, the look in your eye combined with the size of your wager could force players holding much stronger hands to relinquish the pot if you continued to up the ante and bluffed your opponent into withdrawing. Poque spread to the northern states on Mississippi riverboats, where the pronunciation became pokuh, which, as the game migrated north and east, became 'poker.' The rules changed as well. The 52-card deck was introduced around 1837 to accommodate up to 10 players and make for more lucrative pots, and the option to draw three new cards was introduced.

One early problem was that on the lawless, newly-settled lands of those days, skilled and ruthless cardsharps came to dominate much of the action. When they couldn't beat you with marked cards, or with a 'cold deck' presequenced to deal you a losing hand, or with an ace card hidden up their sleeve, they were liable to draw a pistol and take your money that way. For a long time, it seemed that only a scoundrel or a fool would play what was then called 'the cheater's game', and yet it continued to flourish. Poker became universally popular during the Civil War, when soldiers on both sides took up the game, and after the war survivors brought it home with them to every state and territory. Not surprisingly, on the western frontier it was the most popular card game going, and attracted many unsavoury elements. It was from this era, Amarillo Slim explained, that the term 'Dead Man's Hand' came into being. In the town of Deadwood in the Black Hills of the Dakota Territory in 1876, 'Wild Bill' Hickock, the sheriff of the town and an inveterate gambler, was playing in Carl Mann's saloon when an enemy of his, Jack 'Crooked Nose' McCall, sneaked up behind him and shot him in the back of the head with a Colt .45 revolver. Hickock had a fearsome reputation as a gunfighter, so a coward like McCall would never have dared to draw on him face-to-face. As the gambling lawman lay dead, someone noticed that he still had tight hold of his five cards, which included two black aces and two black eights, a combination which has been known ever since as the 'dead man's hand'. No player will bet on such a hand, since it can only bring disaster. Superstition, say some, but nobody ever puts it to the test.

To this day, coloured by its Wild West aura, poker is probably the most popular card game in the world. In the US players still continue to assume cowboy-type names: Amarillo Slim, Texas Dolly, Kid Poker, Oklahoma Johnny. Tournaments have names like Gold Rush, Pot of Gold, Texas Hold 'em Shootout. David Skiansky's books on the strategy of poker, and he has written many of them, all feature smoking Colt revolvers on their cover.

In addition to the usual run of celebrities from Hollywood who frequented the fashionable casinos such as the Sands, the Desert Inn, the Flamingo, Caesar's Palace and so on, the annual invitational Sahara golf tournament attracted scores of the best professional golfers in America to Las Vegas, and with them celebrities from the world of entertainment, to partner them in the pro-am game which preceded the tournament proper. My time at the Horseshoe coincided with a Sahara invitational, and for that week the place was packed with famous golfers who came to sample the gambling atmosphere of the old West at Binion's place. One night at the blackjack table I looked up to see a figure I had seen hundreds of times in the newsreels and sports papers. Standing there was the golfer Lee Trevino, accompanied by a slim, garishly dressed man with a tanned, weather-beaten complexion. They spoke together in Spanish, and Trevino's companion was identified to me as Chi Chi Rodriguez, another golf professional well known on the American circuit. They played a few hands, with smallish stakes as I remember, then wandered off to the craps and roulette tables.

The next morning, on going along to the bookshop to see if I could knock up a game of golf with someone, there, standing at the bar in animated conversation with my new golfing gambler companions, were the two golf professionals, Lee Trevino and Chi Chi Rodriguez. Fast Eddie Seremba introduced them. He, like them, was of Mexican origin, and the two professionals when in Las Vegas always came to the bookshop to meet up with their old friend Fast Eddie for a talk about the old times south of the Rio Grande. As one who was eventually to become twice winner of the British Open, Trevino had played on many British courses, and knew the great Scottish courses well. Since everybody there assumed that as a Scot I must have been an authority on golfing matters, I was drawn into their conversation. Amarillo Slim and Bob Stupak had challenged the two professionals to a match and were trying to arrange a suitable handicap. Now, here you had two high-handicap golfers challenging Lee Trevino, a twice winner-to-be of the British Open and with a string of victories on the American circuit to his name, and a successful American tour golfer, Chi Chi Rodriguez, to a four-ball match-play game and trying to arrange a suitable handicap. I swallowed rapidly when I heard the stakes. They were going to bet $10,000 a man! $40,000 on a friendly game of golf!

I was asked for my opinion as to handicapping. Well, I said, the par on the Desert Inn course was 72. The two professionals were capable of going round in a better-ball score of 60 or even lower. For two 18 to 20 handicappers even to dream about matching such a score, one stroke on the par four, two strokes on the par fives and possibly one stroke on the par threes would have to be given, since neither of them was capable of breaking 95 on a regular basis. If they played at their very best they might achieve a better-ball score of 80. That meant that about 20 strokes or so should be given, making it possible for the two amateurs to approach a better-ball score of around 60 and thus make a game of it.

Arguments raged back and forth. Cries of robbers and bandits rang out and friendly insults were exchanged, and after much argument Trevino came up with another offer. The two amateurs would start on the first tee 15 holes up with 18 to play, he suggested. He and Chi Chi would give them each a stroke a hole. Amarillo and Bob didn't even have to win a hole for victory. Three halved holes in the first 15 would win them the match. As an added concession the game would be played from the middle tees, thus subtracting a good few hundred yards from the length of the course. There was a further long discussion, with the gamblers trying to figure out the odds on the basis of Trevino's offer. Finally, after more argument and calculation that form of handicap was accepted, and I was asked to referee the match.

The first hole at Desert Springs is 445 yards long. Trevino teed up and drove off. He had a somewhat flat, looping swing and always sent the ball low and well off to the left, making it fade into the center of the fairway as it came to the end of its flight, about 250 yards or so down from the tee. Rodriguez had a more orthodox swing, and his ball flew straight as an arrow, to land within a few yards of his partner's. Bob Stupak drove next and lunged at the ball, sending it bumping along the center of the fairway until it came to rest about 190 yards ahead of the tee. Amarillo Slim followed with a stiff upright swing, and his ball landed full pitch into a bunker about 160 yards or so away and half buried itself in the sand. He managed to get it out with his second shot, moving it 80 yards further down the fairway. Stupak hit a fair second shot dead centre, leaving about another 40 or 50 yards to the green. Amarillo connected well with his third and finished about 50 feet from the hole. Rodriguez laid his second shot stiff to the pin, leaving him with a fifteen-footer or so for a birdie. Trevino played his second and his ball came to rest about 25 feet from the hole. Stupak pitched on with his third shot, took two putts and with a stroke off he was down in a par four. Amarillo took three more, down in six, which with a stroke off meant down in five. Rodriguez didn't have to putt. Trevino rattled his ball in, down in a birdie three, and the professionals went to the second tee only fourteen down.

That was the pattern for the rest of the game. To cut a long story very short, the amateurs lost every hole and were able to halve only one. Their 15 up dwindled until they stood on the 17th tee with the professionals one up and two to play. The match finished on the 17th green, Trevino and Rodriguez the victors by two holes. The winnings were handed over in the clubhouse with a handshake and backslapping good humour all round. I suppose the loss of £10,000 on a golf game is no big deal to men used to winning and losing in the hundreds of thousands at the gaming tables. Discussing the match some days later at the bookshop Eddie Seremba remarked to me, 'Lee was never in danger of losing that match. I remember the days ten years or so ago when Lee used to play on Texas courses on a strict handicap basis for a hundred dollars a round when he didn't have a cent in his pocket to pay off if he got beaten. I used to carry his clubs. He never did get beaten. He always won. He had to. They don't take kindly to welshers in Texas.'

By now the bookshop had become the focal point of my spare time and I visited there almost on a daily basis for the stimulating company to be had and to arrange as many golf games as I could get with my new friends. A fairly regular visitor there from his home and golf shop at the La Rinconada course in California was the now very senior Australian golfer Joe Kirkwood, more famous for his amazing trick shots than for his ability to win tournaments. He came to Las Vegas every month or so for two reasons. He liked to gamble a little at the Horseshoe where he had many friends made in the days when he used to tour with his golfing colleague, Walter Hagen, who was also a bit of a gambler, and to pick up a stock of the Luckmans' books on gambling which sold quite well to the customers of his pro shop.

In twenty years of tournament golf, even though he made a good living out of it, Kirkwood never won a single tournament. He was a magnificent striker of the ball from tee to green, but once on the putting surface he was no better than a fifteen handicapper, and unless you can average fewer putts than shots you have no chance of ever winning a golf tournament. In those far-off years on the golf circuit his name would appear in the top ten or twenty prizewinners in the major tournaments of Great Britain and America. In 1925 at Prestwick he came sixth behind the winner, James Barnes. He was just 17 years old at the time. In the Open at St Andrews in 1927 at the age of 19 he finished fourth behind the winner, Bobby Jones. In 1932 at Sandwich he was seventh to Gene Sarazen. In 1934 he came fourth to Henry Cotton at Sandwich and at St Andrews in 1946 he was ninth behind the winner, Sam Snead. After that year his name no longer appeared in the lists of players in the great championships.

The reason was simple. He stopped playing in tournaments. He discovered that he could make a lot more money by doing what he was unparalleled at, the execution of trick shots. At the beginning of each tournament he was paid a flat fee by the organisers to give exhibitions of his mastery of the golf ball, earning as much by his demonstrations as he could have done playing, and without the wear and tear on the nerves. He knew Scotland well from his young days and chatted to me at length about his visits there. He recalled that his last tour of Britain had finished with an exhibition of his shots at a course in Scotland, the Clober course in Milngavie. He was a close friend of Dave Skiansky, and was easily persuaded by him to give a demonstration of his skill at the Desert Inn course. News of this had got out and there was a fair gallery to watch the old master perform his bag of golf tricks. Although fairly on in years and somewhat out of practice he could still amaze.

He could bend the flight of the ball through 180 degrees at will, making it hook or slice and bring the ball back as though it were a boomerang. He could hit two balls within a split second of one another, drawing one in and fading the other out, making it appear as if the two balls would collide in mid-air. He could drive a ball as far with any club in his bag, including the putter, as he could with a driver. He could play a full drive with the ball teed on the face of a watch borrowed from an anxious spectator. He could hole six stymied balls in a row in rapid succession. He could take a full shot at a ball and catch it as it popped up in front of his face. He could hit 12 full tee shots in quick succession straight down the middle of the fairway with a blindfold over his eyes. He could play right-handed shots with a left-handed club and vice versa. He would hammer a ball into the turf until it was barely visible then hit it effortlessly down the fairway for a full two hundred yards with a spoon (3 wood in today's language). At the height of his powers the climax of his repertoire used to be the driving of a ball from a tee held in the mouth of a blonde lying flat on her back, a feat which invariably drew a gasp from the assembled spectators, but he declined to attempt this at the Desert Inn, with the remark that at his age he had no desire to spend the rest of his life in jail for manslaughter!

In 1963 the Ryder Cup was played on a course in Atlanta and the British team was entertained in Las Vegas by the management of the Sahara. In 1967 the Ryder Cup was again played in the USA, this time on a course in Houston, Texas. The American team was captained by the legendary Ben Hogan, and the little Welshman Dai Rees was in charge of the British side. The result was something of the order of 27 games to the Americans and 5 to the British. Not to be outdone by the Sahara hotel four years previously, Dell Web, the owner of the Desert Inn, chartered a plane and flew the entire British team as his guests to enjoy the hospitality of the Desert Inn for a few days and play some golf on the Las Vegas courses. As I remember it, the British team consisted of Peter Alliss, Christy O'Connor, Neil Coles (who made the journey from Houston by car, since he had an inordinate aversion to flying), Brian Huggett, Tony

Jacklin and Dai Rees the captain. The others' names I can't remember offhand. That week saw an invasion of the Hollywood golfing fraternity. Prominent amongst those who greeted the British contingent were Bob Hope and Bing Crosby, both keen golfers who hosted their own tournaments in California, the Bing Crosby Open and the Bob Hope Classic. Fred MacMurray, a tall rugged leading man of that period, arrived in the company of Jack Elam, a character actor who usually played villainous bad-guy western roles. These were all low handicap golfers, the best of them without doubt being Bing Crosby who played off two, with Bob Hope not far behind. Oddly enough, now that I think of it, Crosby and Hope were never seen in any of the gaming rooms at the casinos. The cynics said that Bob Hope was too mean to risk losing a single cent, but I never heard any reason advanced for Crosby's absence.

My Gamblers' Bookshop golfing friends seized on the opportunity and connived to play as many games as they could with the Limeys, whom they all thought were great guys, especially Christy O'Connor, who could outdrink the best of them at the nineteenth hole. In the evening most of the British golfers came to the Sands in the hope of seeing Sinatra's Rat Pack in action, and one or two of them tried their luck at the tables, with Christy O'Connor ahead of them all in sinking the highballs. I never saw a man who could hold his liquor so well, apart from maybe Lee Marvin. The trouble with being Irish is that wherever you go in this world you are going to meet another Irishman, and in Las Vegas there were many of them, all insisting that Christy have a jar on them.

The team's visit led to a memorable occasion for me. Christy O'Connor was the most affable of men and in the clubhouse of the Desert Inn golf course we spoke at length of Glasgow and Scotland and the Ayrshire courses he loved so well. He had once played in the famous Masters at Augusta, which he said was quite the most beautiful inland course he had ever played on, and I mentioned that I would give my eye teeth for a chance to see that particular tournament.

About a month after the team's visit an envelope franked with a British stamp was delivered to me at the Sands. In it was a short note from Christy O'Connor, explaining that tickets for the playing days at the Masters could not be had for love nor money, but that maybe I could put the two enclosed tickets for the practice rounds and for the par-three tournament that preceded the Masters proper to good use. Well, I couldn't have been more pleased if I had won the pools! I sent him off a thank-you letter and couldn't wait to get to the bookshop to show the tickets off. I was immediately everybody's best friend. Who was I going to take with me? That posed a problem. There was only one fair way to do it, since I had no one special friend to favour. Cut cards for it, aces high, and Eddie Seremba won with a king, which pleased me, for I had found him very easy to get on with. Even though the Masters was six months away, in April of 1968, accommodation for that week anywhere in Augusta was hard to find, plus the fact that the Augusta tourist board who had sent us a sheaf of brochures on request, informed us that for Masters week all hotel prices were tripled!

We found a room in a motel about 12 miles from the course and paid for it five months in advance. A few days before Masters week I conveniently developed a sprained wrist, which prevented me from dealing at the tables and allowed me to take time off. The sprain healed quickly during the three days Eddie and I spent tramping the fairways at the Augusta National Course! Those were three days to be remembered. The Augusta course is all that it's cracked up to be, beautifully designed, lush fairways and manicured greens, and the tournament perfectly organized. In retrospect, we were happier watching the practice rounds than we would have been spectating at the tournament proper. More freedom to walk around and a chance to get up close to the players. I sent Christy O'Connor a postcard and drank a jar to his health. The winner of the coveted Masters jacket that year was a little known golfer, Gay Brewer.

THIRTEEN

FAMOUS GAMBLERS

I've never had the pleasure of working in any of the big London or continental casinos, but from what I have heard from dealers who have experienced both the Vegas casinos and places like Crockford's in London and Monte Carlo on the Riviera, the difference is one of ambience and clientele. The card games are the same, and one roulette wheel is much like another, but there the similarity ends. In stark contrast to the gaudily lit and noisy razzmatazz of the American gambling scene, in the traditional European casinos everything is kept dignified and low-key. The croupiers and dealers are polite and impeccably dressed, betting commands are sedately made in French, and there are no gaming machines to lower the tone, or so I'm told. However for some years Monte Carlo has had a pavilion outwith the main building where daytrippers from across the Italian border can feed coins into one-armed bandits with as much noise and enthusiasm as their American counterparts five thousand miles away in Nevada.

Probably as much money passes across the tables in Europe as does in America; the difference lies in the nature of the gambling clientele. Crockford's of London, I am told, sees some of the heaviest gambling to be done anywhere in the world, but the heavy gamblers are quiet, anonymous figures who do not seek publicity, many of them oil-rich Arabs who think nothing of betting hundreds of thousands of pounds on the turn of a roulette wheel or on the deal of a card. Croupiers who have served in these casinos tell me that the Arabs who frequent them seem to have a complete disregard for the value of money; to them it is simply oil flowing from an inexhaustible well.

I can tell of my own experience of such Arab indifference to money. During my time in Majorca (about which in a later chapter), after a game of golf at Son Vida, the 9.30 Golfing Society members used to congregate for a drink at their favourite bar in Son Rapinya, a little one-street town about a kilometre from the Son Vida estate. Whenever I played with them I would join them there at the local bar for a beer. At the entrance to Son Vida, on the left behind a high wall, there stands a huge ornate mansion set well back from the access road. Marble letters spell out its name, 'El Sakrah'. In it lived a sizeable and obviously very wealthy Arab family. Every day, round about noon, a chauffeur-driven Mercedes would emerge from the heavy iron gate and drive the kilometre down to Son Rapinya. The Mercedes would stop in front of our bar and the chauffeur would step down and open the passenger door. Out would step a young Arab boy to walk briskly to the bar counter and ask for a chocolate ice in impeccable Spanish. He always paid for it with a note, sometimes a 1000 peseta note, sometimes a 5000 peseta note. He never waited for the change! 5000 pesetas would have fed a Spanish family of four for a week! Small wonder that when that boy is grown into a man he will think nothing of squandering in one bet a sum of money which my old foreman John McCluskey could not have earned in two lifetimes.

It could well be that if they were ever made known, the exploits of many of these rich Arab gamblers would leave the adventures of the much publicised American casino bank-busters of today in the shade, but the Middle Eastern oil potentates and those of the European aristocracy who gamble heavily do not seek publicity, and they do not perform in the full glare of media attention as their Western counterparts do. It is beyond doubt that it is because of the glamour that surrounds the American gambling scene and the worldwide publicity that has been given to it by the spread of the Hollywood cinema that all the well-known gamblers of the twentieth century seem to be Americans or European immigrants to America.

As far as the visitors to the Luckmans' bookshop were concerned, the centre of the gambling world lay in the western states of the US and in particular the older casinos of Las Vegas. They regarded the bar area of the bookshop much as the members of a golf club regard the club-house lounge, a place to talk golf and all matters related to that game. Over and above being a bookshop, Luckman's was a club where gamblers and dealers congregated to talk shop and to tell tales of the great gamblers of the present and of the past. As far as they were concerned the gambling legends were all to be found in the good old USA. They spoke of Kerry Packer, of course, but implied that if he wasn't American, well, he should be.

Of course, not all were as ignorant of the outside world. Fast Eddie Seremba, the craps player, knew more than most about the history of gambling and could tell of some of the European old-timers who had left their mark in the gambling world. Few, if any, in the bookshop had heard of John Montagu, the Earl of Sandwich, the famous British politician of the eighteenth century whose name became immortal because of his addiction to gambling. To avoid having to leave the gaming tables for a meal when hungry, he would order his servants to bring him a piece of meat between two slices of bread, thus going down in history as the inventor of the sandwich.

Fast Eddie also spoke of a famous French mathematician of the same period, Chevalier de La Mer, a notorious gambler who claimed to have made a fortune by applying an algebraic approach to the laws of probability and who spent the better part of his life in the gambling houses of Paris.

Then there was Fyodor Dostoevsky, the famous Russian novelist who wrote at an amazing speed. He produced two novels of the quality of *The Brothers Karamazov* and *Crime and Punishment* within a twelve-month period but squandered all his wealth at the gaming tables. Dostoevsky wrote a novel *The Gambler*, a penetrating insight into the mind of a compulsive gambler, in just six weeks, so as to pay off a large gambling debt. Fast Eddie's listeners did not pay much attention to his tales about these characters, however. They always seemed to turn the conversation back to the exploits of some Arizona gunslinging poker player who added an extra notch on his six-shooter almost every time he sat down at a card table.

However, they all spoke in reverential terms of Nicholas Andrea Dandolos, or Nick the Greek as he had become known in his adopted country. I have mentioned some of his exploits earlier in this book.

Nick the Greek was born in Crete in 1893 into a wealthy ship-owning family and studied in a theological college in Greece with the intention of becoming a priest. He was not happy with his studies there, so his father sent him to Harvard with an allowance of $150 a week. He fell in with a racy, high-spending gambling crowd, and became a close friend of a leading jockey of the day, Phil Musgrove. He started to bet on horses, and after six months of betting at the racetrack he had won nearly half a million dollars. He did exactly the reverse of what Stu Ungar was destined to do fifty years later. Nick the Greek won on the horses and lost it all in the gaming rooms, playing card and dice games that he was not familiar with and so became fair game for the cardsharps who played against him. But he had a moral fibre that Ungar did not possess. Also, unlike Ungar, he had a rich family to fall back on, so did not take to drink and drugs, but began to study these games in depth, and after a few years he began to acquire a reputation as a solid gambler who seldom failed to win at any game in which he chose to participate. Paradoxically, casino proprietors were glad to lose money to him, for he was such a flamboyant character that he never failed to attract crowds wherever he went, and the losses incurred by ordinary gamblers as they tried to emulate his feats more than made up for his huge winnings.

He was a proud, arrogant man who did not believe that there was anyone capable of beating him at poker, and when the fame of Johnny Moss grew to match his own he asked Benny Binion to arrange a high-stakes poker marathon with the emerging champion. Binion, as described in an earlier chapter, agreed to set up the match at his Horseshoe casino in Las Vegas, with the stipulation that the public should be allowed to watch the game. Benny positioned the gaming table just inside the entrance where it drew large audiences who viewed the action from specially arranged tiered seats. Wealthy hopefuls were allowed to buy in to the game for a minimum of $10,000, but none lasted for any length of time, which is not surprising, given that one of the pots, won eventually by the Greek, amounted to $520,000! It has to be remembered that when the game took place Dandalos was in his sixties and Moss was just approaching his prime, and when a game lasts for five weeks as this one did, then stamina must play a great part in the outcome. Moreover, experienced gambler though he undoubtedly was, Dandalos was playing with his own money, which must have created a certain amount of psychological tension, while Moss had been staked by Binion and would have suffered no personal financial loss in the event of a defeat. However, the fact remains that eventually Dandalos retired after having lost an estimated $2 million, with the famous words, 'Mr Moss, I have to let you go now.' He died in 1963. In the film *The Cincinnati Kid*, made in 1968, the gambler played by Edward G. Robinson is modelled on Dandalos.

Another famous figure never far from the conversation in Luckman's was the notorious Arnold Rothstein, the New York City big-time gambler, bootlegger, and friend of notorious gangsters, high-placed politicians and business men. As far as is known Rothstein never visited the west coast of the US and he had probably never heard of Las Vegas, for at the time of his activities in New York the town that was eventually to become the gambling capital of the western world was still a cluster of wooden shanties in the middle of the Nevada desert. Nevertheless his name is now spoken there with respect as one of the all-time greats of gambling.

Arnold Rothstein was born in 1882 on the east side of New York and grew up in a neighbourhood full of gangs with different racial backgrounds. In his teens he was already involved in gambling and loansharking and, by the 1920s, had cultivated the friendship of politicians and businessmen as well as gang leaders. He became a friend of Big Tim Sullivan, a leading political figure in Tammany Hall, the Irish political organization that controlled all public services in New York, and with that politician's backing he took on the role of City fixer. Rothstein acted as a go-between in business contracts with the city council and was paid handsome sums for his trouble. When necessary he saw to the quashing of arrests and arranged for a blind eye to be turned towards speak-easies, brothels and other criminal enterprises. He was involved in direct brib-ery to politicians and to the police. His well-tailored, well-mannered, quiet look of respectability contrasted with the garishness and vulgarity of such mobsters as Al Capone of Chicago and Vito Genovese of New York, and he became the role model for later heads of organized crime such as Lucky Luciano, Myer Lansky and Frank Costello.

With the huge sums he won at the gaming tables he became a banker for bootlegging and other smuggling enterprises. Cash was needed to buy bootleg liquor in Canada, the Bahamas and Cuba, the three favourite markets for the American gangs to buy their illicit booze in, and Rothstein could supply it through finance houses and banks in these countries, thus eliminating the necessity of carrying large sums of cash in suitcases, a procedure which was risky, to say the least. Rothstein was an independent, had no gang of his own and worked with gangsters of all ethnic groups—Jewish, Italian and Irish—hiring them and selling them favours without discrimination. He decided to open his own gambling house in New York and rented two large apartments in a fashionable district of the city. He and his wife Carolyn took up residence in one, while the other was fitted out with roulette wheels, faro and poker tables. Gambling was of course illegal in New York, but with the help of his friend Big Tim Sullivan, the police authorities were bribed to turn a blind eye and his gambling house became the focal point for all serious gamblers in the New York area.

He then opened a new casino in Hewlett, Long Island, where the cost of 'protection' was not nearly as high as it was in Manhattan. Both the land and the building where the gambling house operated were owned by a New York senator who was a major political figure in national politics. The casino was lavishly furnished and provided the gamblers, who arrived by invitation only, with the best in food and drink. All of the casino's employees were required to dress in appropriate evening wear. Rothstein took advantage of what he termed 'snob appeal' for his gambling den. 'People like to think they're bet-ter than other people,' Rothstein once told Damon Runyon, in whose com-pany he was often seen, and who used him as the model for the character 'Dave the Dude' in some of his immortal stories about life on Broadway. 'As long as they're willing to pay to prove it, I'm willing to let them.' For three years he allowed them to 'pay,' to the tune of $1 million a year in profits, before he was forced to close the club by a newly elected state senator who was too rich to be bribed.

Rothstein had also become active in the horseracing scene and was the person to approach for lay-off betting in the bookmaking business. This is the process of balancing out a bookie's commitments when one horse has had so much money bet on it that a win could break the bookie's bank. The bookie at risk simply splits the bet with someone with enough money to handle the risk and the two share any winning percentage from the bets placed. This involves access to large sums of money in the event of a loss and by the 1920s Rothstein's huge cash reserves allowed him to set the terms for such bets. Soon he became known from coast to coast as the man who could handle any lay-off bet, no matter how high the amount involved.

Rothstein's favourite eating-place was Lindy's restaurant on Seventh Avenue, a venue that was to be made famous by the stories of Damon Runyon. There he had a private booth which also served him as an office. He kept a regular schedule in the restaurant and several men were waiting to see him when he walked in one night in November 1928. He left early, saying that he had been invited to a high-stakes poker game at the Park Central Hotel. Present at the game were several well-known New York big-time gamblers: Nate Raymond, Alvin 'Titanic' Thompson—so called because he had survived the sinking of the *Titanic*—and Joe Bernstein, a close friend of the gangster Myer Lansky. The game began on November 8th and continued into the morning of November 10th. By the end of the marathon card game, Rothstein had lost considerable amounts of money. He owed Raymond $219,000, Bernstein $73,000, and Thompson $30,000. The circumstances of the climax of that game were never made public, but suddenly a shot rang out and seconds later a revolver was thrown out of the hotel room window and landed on the roof of a taxi in the street below. It had been wiped clean of fingerprints. Rothstein had been shot and badly wounded in the stomach and died two days later in hospital, without naming his killer. His funeral was attended by thousands of mourners and he lies buried in the Jewish Cemetery at Union Field in the Queens district of New York.

Amarillo Slim's gambling hero was the famous sheriff Bat Masterson, who, according to the champion poker player, was the first man to open a proper gambling casino in the West. Bat Masterson was born in Illinois in the second half of the nineteenth century. He got his first job at seventeen as a guard on the Atchison, Topeka & Santa Fe railroad. Shortly afterwards, he became a buffalo hunter supplying meat to the railroad crews and then served for a while as a scout for the US cavalry. In 1880, Bat killed his first white man at Sweetwater, Texas (God alone only knows how many Indians he had killed before that incident) and was arrested by the famous Wyatt Earp, who released him when told that Masterson had killed the man in defence of a barmaid. He worked for a spell as a deputy marshal under Wyatt Earp, and was sent by him in that capacity to Dodge City, a wild, lawless frontier town. While there, he purchased an interest in the Lone Star dance hall and equipped it with something never seen in the West before, a roulette table. This created a sensation amongst gamblers, who queued up to play at it. He ran Dodge City with an iron hand and was promoted to the post of US Marshal. He was involved in the famous war between the Denver & Rio Grande and the Atchison, Topeka & Santa Fe railroads for the rights to build a railtrack from the eastern States to Deadwood in South Dakota. Masterson and his posses protected crews of both railroads from being killed in shoot-outs. That year he lost his bid for re-election, and so devoted his time to his Lone Star dance hall where he dealt at cards and faro. He was called to a town called Tombstone, where his friend Wyatt Earp was having problems with the notorious Clanton Gang, but arrived too late to help out at the famous OK Corral incident.

For the next few years he drifted from town to town, following the boomtowns and cow towns, but always kept his interest in the Lone Star saloon. He spent time in Dodge City, Denver, Reno, Las Vegas and Trinidad, of all places. Somewhere along the way he developed an interest in boxing. Although he himself never boxed, he frequently acted as a timekeeper, promoter, second, or referee. He bought the Palace Variety Theater in Denver, turned it into a gambling house and at the same time he wrote a weekly sports column for a Denver paper. He opened the Olympic Athletic Club in Denver to promote boxing, and in the late 1890s he promoted a fight for the heavyweight championship of the world between Gentleman Jim Corbett and the Englishman Bob Fitzsimmons, who was several stones lighter than Corbett. Masterson bet every penny he had on Corbett to win, and lost it all when Corbett was KO'd by the Englishman. Penniless, he went east to New York, where he took up a position as Sports Editor for the *Morning Post*. He died there at the age of 67, in 1921.

I listened fascinated to all these stories and asked on one occasion if there had been any women gamblers of note. Women dealers and croupiers were beginning to appear on the scene in the big glitzy casinos of Las Vegas. They were invariably highly attractive, and drew punters to their tables like bees to a honey pot, the psychology behind it being that men liked to show off to them, placing large bets they would never have dreamed of making if a man were in charge of the table. In all my years as a dealer I had never come across a heavy woman punter. Dave Skiansky, who prided himself as being the historian of the group, had to think hard before he came up with a couple of names.

Poker Alice was the name given to Alice Ivers, who in her lifetime also had the names Duffield, Tubbs and Huckert from her three dead husbands. Two of them were professional gamblers who made a living going from town to town in Texas, Nevada and Colorado early in the twentieth century playing in whatever card game they could find in the saloons and gambling dens along the way. She was always at her husband's side, but didn't seem to bring either of them much luck, because both men were shot dead in arguments at the card table. She married again, this time to a non card-playing gunfighter called Huckert, who stood by her at the tables as she took up where her two dead husbands had left off. She had a phenomenal memory and excelled at faro, blackjack and poker, and made far more money at the tables than her two dead husbands ever had. At the age of 79 in 1932 she became ill while playing in a poker game in Las Vegas. She was rushed to a hospital in Los Angeles where an operation was carried out for a gall bladder condition. She died on the operating table.

His second nomination was Martha Jane Burke, a lady better known as Calamity Jane, who roamed the western frontier during the last part of the nineteenth century. She was renowned for her exploits as a dancehall girl (as hookers were known as in those days), and as camp follower and lover of Wild Bill Hickok. She was also a talented card player and would sit in on any game she happened to come across, where she could match any male in toughness and richness of vocabulary. She captured the imagination of the magazine feature writers of the day who travelled the West in search of material, and became famous when she toured with the Wild West Shows of Buffalo Bill. She finished her days in Deadwood in 1903 and is buried there beside her beloved Wild Bill Hickok.

If a question about leading women gamblers were to be asked nowadays, a list as long as your arm would be supplied, including the winner of the World Poker Championships of the year 2000. The winner in a field of 245 entrants, 95% of them men, was a Mrs Jerri Thomas, wife and mother, who emerged victorious to the tune of $1,414,000. Women now have their own Poker Championship tournament, won in the year 2002 by Sheila Ryan, a New York policewoman.

Framed and hung on one of the walls of the Gamblers' Bookshop is the following remarkable piece of writing. It is dated Rawhide, Nevada, 1908. It is the eulogy to a dead gambler called Riley Grannan, spoken by his friend Herman Knickerbocker, a Baptist minister turned mining prospector. It was delivered over the open coffin which lay in the back room of the saloon where Riley Grannan had been killed in a gunfight. It was written down by a stenographer who happened to be on the scene, and it was published in a Nevada newspaper, the *Territorial Enterprise*. As a party piece Dave Skiansky can recite it from memory. It is an amazing *tour de force*, with quotations from Shakespeare, Omar Khayyam and Dante, joined together with a flow of philospohical speculation. It came from the lips of one who, in his own words, can claim only to be a simple prospector. It is a long piece, running to several thousand words. Some of the passages are reproduced here:

'I feel that it is incumbent upon me to state that in standing here I occupy no ministerial or prelatic position. I am simply a prospector who makes no claims whatever to moral merit or to religion except the religion of humanity, the brotherhood of man. I stand among you today simply as a man among men, feeling that I can shake hands and say "brother" even to the vilest man or woman that ever lived. If there should come to you anything of moral admonition through what I may say, it comes not from any sense of moral superiority, but from the depth of my experience.

Riley Grannan was born in Paris, Kentucky, about 40 years ago. I suppose he dreamed all the dreams of boyhood. At times during his life they blossomed into phenomenal success along financial lines. I am told that from the position of a bell-boy in a hotel he rose rapidly to become a celebrity of world-wide fame. He was one of the greatest plungers, probably, that the continent has ever produced. He died the day before yesterday in Rawhide.

He was born in the sunny Southland, where brooks and rivers run musically through the luxuriant soil; where the magnolias like white stars grow in a firmament of green; where crystal lakes dot the greensward and the softest summer breezes dimple the wave-lips into kisses for the lilies on the shore; where the air is resonant with the warbled melody of a thousand sweet-voiced birds and redolent of the perfume of many flowers. This was the beginning. The end was in Rawhide, where in the winter the shoulders of the mountains are wrapped in garments of ice and in summer the blistering rays of the sun beat down upon the skeleton ribs of the desert. Is this a picture of universal human life?

Sometimes when I look over the circumstances of human life, a curse rises to my lips. When I see the ambitions of man defeated; when I see him struggling with mind and body in the only legitimate prayer he can make to accomplish some end; when I see his aim and purpose frustrated by a fortuitous combination of circumstances over which he has no control; when I see the outstretched hand, just about to grasp the flag of victory, take instead the emblem of defeat, I ask: What is life? Dreams, awakening and death; "a pendulum 'twixt a smile and a tear"; "a momentary halt within the waste and then the nothing we set out from"; "a walking shadow, a poor player that struts and frets his hour upon the stage and then is heard no more"; "a tale told by an idiot full of sound and fury, signifying nothing"; a mockery, a sham, a lie, a vision; its happiness but Dead Sea apples; its pain the crunching of a tyrant's heel.

I know that there are those who will condemn him. There are those who believe today that he is reaping the reward of a misspent life. There are those who are dominated by medieval creeds. To those I have no words to say in regard to him. Such folk are ruled by the skeleton hand of the past and fail to see the moral beauty of a character lived outside their puritanical ideas. His goodness was not of that type, but of the type that finds expression in a word of cheer to a discouraged brother; the type that finds expression in friendship, the sweetest flower that blooms along the dusty highway of life; the type that finds expression in manhood.

But did you ever stop and think how God does not put all his sunbeams into corn, potatoes and flour? Did you ever notice the prodigality with which He scatters these sunbeams over the universe? Contemplate:

God flings the auroral beauties around the cold shoulders of the North; paints the quivering picture of the mirage above the pa]pitating heart of the desert; scatters the sunbeams like lamellated gold upon the bosoms of myriad lakes that dot the verdant robe of nature; spangles the canopy of night with star-jewels and silvers the world with the reflected beams from Cynthia's mellow face; hangs the gorgeous crimson curtain of the Occident across the sleeping-room of the sun; wakes the coy maid of dawn to step timidly from her boudoir to climb the steps of the Orient and fling wide open the gates of the morning. Then, tripping o'er the landscape, kissing the flowers in her flight, she wakes the birds to herald with their music the coming of her King, who floods the world with refulgent gold. Wasted sunbeams, these?

We stand at last in the presence of the Great Mystery. I know nothing about it, nor do you. We may have our hopes, but no knowledge. I do not know whether there be a future life or not; I do not say there is not. I simply say I do not know. I have watched the wicket-gate closed behind many and many a pilgrim. No word has come back to me. The gate remains closed. Across the chasm is the gloomy cloud of death. And now the time has come to say good-bye. The word "farewell" is the saddest in our language. And yet there are sentiments sometimes that refuse to be confined in that word. I will say, "Good-bye, old friend."

If one goes a little deeper into the origins of this rather flowery piece of writing its appearance in an obscure Western town newspaper might not seem so surprising. Just north of Las Vegas lies a mining ghost town, Virginia City.

Virginia City was the home of the Comstock Lode, probably the richest gold and silver mine ever discovered. The gold strike was made in 1860 attracted thousands of prospectors from all over America, and made of Virginia City one of the roughest and bawdiest towns of the old West. The area produced vast quantities of gold and silver until the lode ran dry in the early 1900s and Virginia City was abandoned to become one of the dozens of ghost towns that litter the Nevada and Arizona desert.

Devotees of the Western film will have seen Virginia City many times, for it has often been used as a film set for the dozens of Westerns made in that part of the Nevada desert. On the main street there is a deserted newspaper office and on it a plaque reads:

> To the memory of Mark Twain, who greatly enriched the literature of the West. He started his career as a writer in this building in 1862 as the editor of this newspaper, the *Territorial Enterprise*.

The plaque is signed by a H. Knickerbocker.

FOURTEEN

CASINO MAJORCA

The two years in Las Vegas were not long in passing, given all the activity I had managed to cram into that time. I had enjoyed working in some of the main casinos, especially Binion's Horseshoe and the Sands. I had enjoyed the golf with my bookshop companions at the Desert Inn and Lake Mead courses, and the visit of the British Ryder Cup team followed by my unexpected visit to the Masters in Augusta were occasions I would never forget. I had been home only twice during my two years in Nevada; Rose's letters kept counting the days to my return to Glasgow and as the end of my contract drew near I began thinking about returning to a permanent job with the Stakis casinos. To be quite honest about it, after the experiences of the last two years I did not relish the idea of working in Glasgow again. I had got used to the good life in Nevada. Perfect weather all year round, with a well-paid job and good accommodation and a variety of interesting companions. I kept hinting to Rose in my letters that she might like to emigrate to the States. Las Vegas was expanding and attractive housing estates were springing up around the Lake Mead area. I could apply for a permanent work permit and we could make a good life for the children there, but my Rose would not hear of it. There was no way she would ever leave Glasgow and take the kids away from their school and their friends, she said, that was that, and she wanted to hear no more about it. Besides, what would I do in Nevada when my dealing days were over, she asked. Get a job as a cowboy?

Two weeks before the end of my Vegas contract I was called into the agency office for a word with Pete, the one who had met us on our arrival in Vegas. Although I had already made it plain to him that I no longer wanted to stay in Vegas, he had another offer which might interest me, he said. A Spanish-American consortium was planning to open a number of casinos in mainland Spain, and on the Balearic island of Majorca. One had already opened in Puerto Banus, a posh new marina near Malaga in mainland Spain and the one in

Majorca, built right on the sea at a place called Cala Figuera about 20 kilometres from the capital, Palma, was due to open in about six months time. The Casino Majorca was to be the last word in luxury and the consortium were hoping to attract big spenders from the Mediterranean gambling set, in particular the Arabs, who had money to burn and were building large luxurious mansions for themselves in an area known as Son Vida on the outskirts of Palma. To make access easy for the Mediterranean millionaire yachting set a series of jetties had been built in the tiny bay at the foot of the cliff where the casino stood, and these were to be connected to the casino by means of spectacular elevators, glass-fronted to give a magnificent view of the bay of Palma. There was to be no hotel attached to the casino, but a five-star restaurant was to be part of the complex and the consortium were planning that it should be the jewel in their gambling crown.

The casino was to be staffed by hand-picked dealers, the best available, and since my contract was now ended, Pete said I might consider a further year's work in Majorca with my present wages, with an option to renew at the end of the year. Accommodation would be provided for myself and my family in the form of a fully-furnished seaside bungalow set next to the casino. I thought about it. The offer certainly sounded good. I had never set foot on Majorca, although the cruise ships I had worked on sometimes dropped anchor there. The new casino as described to me sounded like an exciting place to work in and the perks that went with it were more than attractive. Pete agreed to wait for my answer until I could get back to Glasgow and consult with Rose.

But how could I convince her? She practically went for me with a rolling pin when I first broached the subject to her. I had promised her, she cried, but at long last I got her to listen to the proposition. Firstly I swore on a stack of bibles that this would definitely be my last year abroad, honestly it would. Then I explained the advantages of the accommodation that went with the job. The opening of the casino would coincide with the beginning of school summer holidays, and she and the kids could come and spend the full six weeks with me. We could have a marvellous time all together there, with the beautiful weather we could expect in a place like Majorca, I reasoned. The island was only a couple of hours or so away from Glasgow by plane, and with the growth of tourism there were lots of direct flights available almost every day. Then when the holidays finished wouldn't it be great to get away from the cold and miserable Glasgow winter whenever she wanted? I kept on and on, until reluctantly at first, then quite enthusiastically as she thought more about it, Rose agreed, provided that this would be absolutely and definitely my last job abroad, so I crossed my heart and hoped to die and kissed her and swore that Glasgow would be my next and final stop.

Five weeks later, Rose and I and the three kids were lounging under a huge sunshade on the little patio of our new home in Cala Figuera, sipping drinks as we took in the magnificent view of the shimmering blue sea beneath us and listened to the happy shrieks of the children splashing about in the swimming pool. The casino was only a few yards away and even though it was not yet open for business I was kept busy each day with the rest of the casino staff helping in the installation of the three roulette wheels and the positioning of the nine card tables. The setting was quite magnificent. One side of the gambling room consisted of a window the full width of the building and through it could be seen the wide bay of Palma, with the full spread of the city laid out in panorama. The décor was completely different from anywhere I had ever worked. Gone were the heavy carpets, plush curtains and crystal chandeliers which usually formed part of the fittings of the traditional casino and we were miles away from the razzamataz of the Vegas Strip. Here there were marble floors, tinted mirrors, subdued indirect lighting, and cascading fountains of water in the four corners of the gambling area, creating an ambience of grace and beauty.

But then, with everything in place and just a week before the date of the gala opening, a bombshell fell. Someone discovered that the jetties and lifts provided for the arrival of luxury yachts could never be put to use. The harbour authorities had produced maps which showed that about 500 metres out from the deep water of the bay there existed a rocky shelf which made the waters above it too shallow to allow the passage of anything except the smallest of craft. You would have thought that with all the millions spent on planning someone would have made sure that access from the sea for large craft was possible, but with typical Mallorquin inefficiency the mistake had been made and the dream of an invasion of a wealthy armada from the marinas of the Med evaporated. Casino Majorca opened as scheduled, but in a distinctly low-key manner, with its customers made up of the local population and of tourists from the local package holiday resorts, whose spending power obviously did not justify the amount of money invested. The place was certainly packed to overflowing, but instead of the stakes of hundreds of thousands of pesetas expected by the management, I was spinning the roulette wheel to bets of a few hundred placed by giggling, beer-guzzling Glasgow Fair holidaymakers from Magaluf who seemed to regard the casino as just another amusement arcade.

Not that it mattered all that much to me. My wages were there at the end of the month no matter what the clientele was like, although any dreams I might have had about colossal tips from free-spending sheiks had evaporated. Other events began to compensate for that, however. One night as I was dealing at a half-occupied baccarat table, a vaguely familiar figure sat down before me. The tall, expensively dressed man spoke with a broad Glasgow accent as he asked me to change a few thousand pesetas into chips. He leaned over the table, his Rolex-encased wrist plainly visible.

'The last time I saw you was at the Chevalier a few years back. What brings you to Majorca?'

Right away I remembered Joe Docherty, the Cowcaddens bookie who used to spend a lot of time in the Chevalier, although, being a very wise and successful bookie, he bet little if at all and used the place more as a restaurant and meeting place than a casino, as I recalled. We exchanged a few pleasantries about the old days in Glasgow and after drawing a few indifferent cards and the loss of a few thousand pesetas he left. A few hours later, my shift finished, and with the kids in bed, Rose and I sat at a café table enjoying the soft night air, sipping a drink and watching the world go by.

'Mind if I join you?'

Introductions were made and Joe Docherty pulled up a chair and sat down beside us. He came often to Majorca, he explained, and now that he was retired he came for months at a time to play golf at the nearby Santa Ponsa and Son Vida golf courses. Did I play? Would I like a game? And so early next morning I found myself in the sumptuously appointed locker room of the Son Vida course trying on a borrowed pair of golf shoes and testing the balance of a hired set of clubs. He had filled me in about the background of the course.

After the end of the war with Germany and Japan, the US began looking for bases in the Mediterranean, and Majorca was chosen as a possible site. A small contingent of military surveyors, commanded by Captain Steve Cusak of the US Air Force, arrived there in 1946 to begin a survey of the territory. Cusak, who hailed from California and was married to a Mexican wife, spoke fluent Spanish. He was struck by the natural untouched beauty of the place, and seeing the potential for development he decided to make an investment. While still a soldier he was, of course, not permitted any business activities, but with his wife as a figurehead he began to buy up large tracts of land in the Son Vida valley just north of Palma. The valley was an arid and seemingly worthless expanse of ground surrounded by scrub-covered hills and surmounted by a huge abandoned castle, and before long Cusak was the owner of about 5000 acres of land acquired for a ridiculously small sum from owners who were only too glad to be rid of unproductive fallow land not fit even for the raising of goats. But Cusak now knew something that they did not. His survey had shown that the valley sat on top of a huge underground stream of water, which could be brought to the surface by means of artesian wells. Water in Majorca was, and still is, as precious as oil. There are no rivers on the island, rainfall is amongst the lowest in the Mediterranean, and the limited agriculture had been made possible only by the water brought to the surface by pumps activated by the primitive windmills that dotted the plains north of Palma. The availability of water was the yardstick by which the value of land in Majorca was assessed, and the value of a field could rocket a hundredfold upon the discovery of a source of irrigation.

Very soon in 1948 after his release from the air force, Cusak had set up a development company with three others besides himself as shareholders; a local *alcalde* (mayor), a prominent banker and an ex-colonel of the Spanish army, a mix which guaranteed political, military, and financial leverage. Funds were raised, the necessary permits and the latest in drilling machinery obtained, and in no time the land was growing green, irrigated by the precious water which now literally spewed from the ground. Cusak was far-seeing and had noted the beginning of the post-war tourist boom which was to make the island rich. He raised more capital, restored the ruined castle and made it into a five-star hotel, the Son Vida, which was soon to be filled to capacity by wealthy holidaymakers from northern Europe and Britain. The weather was as good as guaranteed and things were dirt cheap in Spain then. A first-class meal could be had for a couple of quid, a bottle of the local wine, rough though it was, was to be had for five shillings, and spirits were literally cheaper than water, so people of all classes came in droves to visit the new holiday paradise. Inspired by the example of the golfing estates he had known in his native California, Cusak then embarked on the building of a golf course next to the hotel, with the area round the course put on sale in the form of plots of house-building land. Each plot was of 2000 square metres, strict building specifications were laid down and palatial houses soon sprang up, built by oil-rich Arabs, English tax exiles and wealthy Spaniards. By 1965, in the space of fifteen years, one of the most select residential areas in Europe had been created.

Majorca even then had a large and permanent English population. Retired families found that they could live like lords in Majorca and indulge in a lifestyle not available to them in the UK. This expatriate colony welcomed the appearance of the Son Vida golf course and soon commandeered it as their own. Golf was practically unknown in Spain then, Ballesteros had yet to arrive on the scene to make golf the 'in thing' among the Spanish moneyed classes, so the English and a handful of Americans had the course almost to themselves.

Almost, that is, for soon 'undesirable elements' in the form of German and Spanish golfers had begun to infiltrate, and steps were immediately taken to consolidate the Anglo-American golfing ascendancy. The Son Vida 9.30 Golfing Society was formed, with Cusak, himself a keen golfer, as honorary president. The membership of the society was limited to 30 golfers, with all membership by invitation of the committee only, and since the committee consisted of Allen Martin Jenkins, a retired Brigadier, Arthur Lomax, ex-governor of the Sudan, Gibson McCabe, retired chairman of *Newsweek*, Count John de Pret, an Anglo-Belgian Count, and George Turner, retired managing director of the Rootes car group, exclusivity was assured. The first tee was reserved for one hour for the society from 9.30 on all days except Sunday, and a Majorcan golfing institution that was to last for nearly 30 years was born.

Joe Docherty had visited Majorca in the early sixties at the start of his retirement, had fallen in love with the island, and had decided to buy an apartment there for use during the winter months. A keen golfer since pre-war days and still playing to a handicap of four, Joe was immediately attracted to the sun-bathed fairways of the Son Vida golf course, and since membership was to be had simply on application, a year's subscription was paid and Joe began a daily visit to his new club. Given that the 9.30 Society had the tee reserved for one hour in the mornings, it irked him somewhat to have to wait until 10.30 to seek a game, for that meant a late finish well into the afternoon, the speed of play in Majorca being as slow as it was.

It had never crossed his mind to approach the plummy-voiced group of Englishmen who assembled so possessively on the tee just after nine o'clock for a game, for to someone reared in Glasgow there was something inherently alien in the affectations of their upper-class English voices. By this time the 9.30 Society had become somewhat thin in the ranks; age and a surfeit of the cheap wine and gin readily available in Majorca had put paid to some, and as the cost of living began to keep pace with the island's growing prosperity others had decided to return to their native England where the National Health Service could be relied upon to minister to the needs of their advancing years. The society was now down to 18 members, this even after the strict membership standards of its early days had been relaxed. Even a Frenchman had been allowed in! He was Bernard Mahe, a retired racing driver, with a Mille Miglia victory and a second in both the Monza trials and the Targa Florio under his belt, who could speak reasonable English, and could play a fair game of golf.

At all costs the encroaching and ever more numerous German visitors had to be kept at bay, as had the newly emerging Spanish golfers with their very elastic interpretation of the rules and complete lack of course etiquette, so to help keep up numbers Mahe was enrolled in the society, even though he insisted on bringing his dog along during games. His pet was a poodle, of all things, and was led along on a leash by the Frenchman's caddy. The poodle was well-enough behaved, but had the nasty habit of peeing up against golf bags, which did not endear Mahe to his fellow golfers.

I had been well filled in as to the history of the group; they were beginning to gather in the vicinity of the tee and I sized them up with interest as we prepared to tee off in the slot just before 9.30. We were playing a threesome, since Joe had invited along a fellow bookie from Glasgow, his friend and frequent companion at the Chevalier, Jimmy McLean of the misplaced Caserta fortune, who had come to Majorca for a fortnight's holiday. I drove off first and hit a fairish ball down the middle. Joe went next and rifled a cracker thirty or forty yards past mine, and then Jimmy McLean stepped onto the tee. His first contact with the English group was not a happy one. As Jimmy was getting ready to drive to a background of suitable silence from the onlookers, Mahe's poodle appeared at the edge of the box led by a young caddy, and promptly cocked its leg ready to pee on the bookie's golf bag. Jimmy poked at it with his driver.

'Get that effin' dug away!'

Although the Glasgow accent might have been incomprehensible, the motion of the club and the menace in the voice were not, and the caddy yanked the dog away, to the consternation of Mahe, who immediately leaned over to console his affronted pet while throwing a dark look at the stranger who had dared chastise his poodle.

'Shoudnay huv a bluddy dug on the course anyway,' continued Jimmy, and rifled a long drive smack down the middle of the fairway. Joe and Jimmy were both low-handicap golfers and the quality of their play was not lost on John de Pret, the captain of the society, who followed us onto the tee and who, given the slowness of the play, could observe us on almost every subsequent hole. He had often seen Joe from afar on the course, but this was the first time he had been able to take stock of him at close range.

De Pret was a huge man of about 50 years of age, son of a Belgian count and English mother, a hard-drinking, hard-smoking expatriate who had lived on the island for about 15 years in semi-luxurious ease, thanks to a remittance cheque which arrived each month from his family in England. He was a fine golfer, especially when fuelled by several large draughts of gin or whisky, and he could see in the players ahead of him three potential recruits for his beloved society if their backgrounds did not deviate too much from the entrance requirements. He began to exchange pleasantries with us during the long wait on each tee. Joe and Jimmy could moderate their Glasgow patter at will and I could speak plain English as well if I had to, and soon names and identities and backgrounds were exchanged in a common language, if not a common accent. That afternoon, after the morning's golf, the committee sat and discussed the question of whether the three Scots should be invited into the 9.30 Society. John de Pret was nothing if not pragmatic. The existing members could not take up the all the allocated time on the tee. As the members continued to diminish in number, which was inevitable, that time would be shortened, and there might follow an encroachment of Germans and Spaniards into the morning's play, a development which was to be avoided at all costs, he argued, even if it meant inviting two Glasgow bookies and a casino croupier into their august circle. Besides, they were bloody good golfers, especially the bookies, and knew the game better than most, which could only be to the advantage of their circle. Besides, they had taken the correct approach to Mahe's dog on the first tee. Pity they hadn't done the bloody nuisance in! Counter arguments were put forward. The exclusiveness of the original group had been diluted far enough, some said. The Frenchman with his poodle was about as far down the scale as one could go, and the idea of admitting a couple of rather uncouth and obviously vulgarly rich Glaswegians—both of them bookies, no less—together with a rather tough-looking casino employee, was simply not on. And who would the newcomers invite to play with them? More of the same ilk, no doubt.

But they were good golfers, said others, a damn sight better than most of us, and we do need new blood after all. So a vote was taken, the motion that the three newcomers to Son Vida be invited to join the society was passed, and the next morning the invitation to join was given to the three of us by John de Pret. We looked at one another. What did membership entail? A small subscription? No problem there. Weekly competitions amongst themselves and the occasional match with visiting groups from England? That sounded like fun. Monthly lunches for the members and one grand ladies' night each year? The women might like that. I imagined that Rose certainly would, and so the three of us agreed to become members of the 9.30 Society. From then on Joe and Jimmy and I formed part of the group assembled on the first tee at Son Vida each morning, our Glasgow accents now prominent amongst the plummy English tones of our new golfing companions.

We were introduced individually to the members by John de Pret, the society captain. A croupier at the new Cala Figuera Casino? Another Scot ? I could see the look of disdain on some of the members' faces. The majority were pleasant enough, though, and plied me with questions about the new casino.

'Must come along for a flutter some night.'

And indeed they did. They were anything but heavy gamblers, betting a few hundred pesetas on the wheel and at the card tables, but at least they made the place look busy.

After the summer holidays, with Rose and the kids back in Glasgow, I played with the group three times each week and enjoyed every minute I spent on the fairways of the Club de Golf de Son Vida, away from the boring and uninspiring atmosphere of the casino. On the whole the 9.30 Society members were a pleasant and decent lot once you got used to the English mannerisms and accents, and I began to look forward to my games with them. To promote familiarity amongst members and to bring variety into the morning pairings, all new members were allotted a different partner for each round by the captain. Some I enjoyed playing with, some I did not. My favourite partner, apart from my two Glasgow bookie friends, was Bernard Metcalf, a retired printer from Birmingham, who despite his 60 or so years could still play a fair game of golf and was himself of a working-class background. Jimmy McLean's preferred partner was, of all people, retired Brigadier Alan Martin Jenkins, late of the 8th Indian division of the British army. Two more different characters it would be hard to imagine, one the polished and suave product of Sandhurst, and the other the rough Glasgow street bookie with a rather thin veneer of education. They had one thing in common, however. They had both fought for six months at the Battle of Monte Cassino and had a world of shared experiences to talk about. Unfortunately the Brigadier was of no help to Jimmy in suggesting a solution to the lost Caserta fortune!

The person I least enjoyed playing with, in common with almost all the other members, was Major Tom Lyon, late of the 3rd Ghurka rifle battalion attached to Orde Wingate's Chindits. He certainly had an impressive war record, but as a golfing partner the retired Major was someone to be avoided. He was stone deaf, and compensated for this by conversing with his partner in a parade-ground voice which carried across at least three fairways. His conversation, which was more of a monologue, since he could not hear any reply from his companion, was somewhat repetitive and consisted of stories of his exploits along the Irrawaddy river, which when heard once or twice were certainly interesting, but palled somewhat with constant repetition. Moreover, he was the slowest player imaginable, for he could not bear to lose a ball, a fixation which invariably caused long delays on a course where one could easily lose a ball on every hole if the fairway was missed. He would insist on spending all the time necessary to find his ball in the rough, and would not continue play until a ball, not necessarily his own, was found by his caddy. His old companions in the society were well aware of this idiosyncrasy, and to keep play flowing supplied his caddy with half a dozen or so balls to be conveniently found when a reasonable time had elapsed in a fruitless search for the Major's wildly struck ball. I was introduced to him by John de Pret.

'Morrison, Morrison', repeated the Major. 'We had a Morrison in our battalion. Copped his lot in Johor Baru. Any relation of yours, by any chance?'

He paid no heed to my disclaimer but went into a long description of the action where the lamented Morrison had copped his lot. Somehow I survived my first game with the Major and made a mental note to avoid a repetition of the experience if at all possible. One morning soon after I had joined the society the Major decided to have a bit of practise on his own before his companions arrived and walked on to the 14th. tee adjoining the clubhouse, meaning to play that hole and then the 18th, which led back to the first tee. Since there were as yet no golfers on the course and no caddies available, he put a few clubs into a pencil bag, slung it over his shoulder and followed his drive down the fairway. The 14th safely negotiated, he walked onto the 18th tee and surveyed the hole. The 18th was probably the most difficult hole on the course. It was a dog-leg to the left of some 475 yards, and the ball had to be hit along a sloping fairway which could gather up even a well-struck ball and run it into a long lake which ran half the length of the hole.

The Major teed up his ball, aimed well to the right of the fairway so as to eliminate the danger of the water hazard and hit a long hook, which cleared the fairway and splashed into the water at the edge of the lake. He picked up his bag of clubs, walked down to the edge and saw his ball lying clearly in what seemed to be just a few feet of water. He knelt down, selected a suitable club from the bag, and leaned over to fish the ball out. His first attempt knocked the ball further away and as he leaned over further, he lost his balance and toppled into the still waters of the lake. The water there was deeper than it had appeared, coming nearly up to his neck as his feet touched the bottom. He waded over to the grass verge and attempted to pull himself out. To no avail. He kept slipping back down the steep moss-covered cement bank of the hazard, and try as he might could not get out and back onto the fairway. He paused for a moment and shouted for help at the top of his voice, but the sound failed to carry back to the first tee where some early morning golfers were preparing to tee off.

That same morning I too had decided to have a few early practice holes, and as I walked along by the lake on the 18th I heard a faint voice calling for help. I looked, and there was the Major, up to his neck in water, waving frantically at me. I managed to pull him back onto the fairway, soaked and covered in water and weeds, but none the worse for wear from his twenty-minute or so immersion in the lake. Fuming with chagrin, he walked back to the clubhouse where he changed into dry clothes, and began his belated round of golf to the accompaniment of unsympathetic comments from his friends, the consensus of their remarks being that he should have been left to drown where he was!

It was not until he arrived at the third hole and went to pick a nine iron from his bag that he realised that the club had vanished into the lake, where it remained lost, together with the only ball he had ever failed to find in all his years of playing on Son Vida.

The culmination of the golfing year was the gala ladies night, held in the La Vileta restaurant on the outskirts of Palma, a rambling hacienda-style place owned by Bob Edwards, a young Welshman who had lived most of his life in Majorca and who occasionally played as a guest with the 9.30 Society. The affair was planned each year by Bernard Metcalf, who regularly designed striking invitations and menus for the event. This gala night was due to be held just a few weeks after our joining; I attended with Rose, we had a marvellous time, and I could see that she was beginning to take to the Majorcan way of life.

During the summer months in Majorca the area near and around the casino is practically taken over by holidaymakers from Glagow, so it was not too great a surprise when I saw Tommy Reid walk into the gaming room one night. About ten years or so older than I was, Tommy Reid was someone I knew well. I'll use that name because he might not like me to mention his real one. His family lived a few closes up from us in Willock Street and our respective mothers had been great friends. His young days had been no different from those of anyone else in that neighbourhood; rough and ready and fend for yourself. Even as a teenager he had an eye for a quick bob or two, and had started to lay the foundation for his future fortune early in life. Together with one or two other enterprising chaps from the neighbourhood he had started off in the lucrative business of stripping lead from tenement roofs and selling it to scrap metal dealers. This was a dangerous business to be in on two counts. You could fall off the roof and break your neck, or you could get nicked by the polis and spend a month or so in jail. Tommy had been both very able and very lucky in his enterprise. Neither of these two fates had befallen him, but soon he had acquired his own scrap metal business, then expanded into the demolition trade and over the years had become one of the richest men in the Glasgow area.

A few years back I had been able to do Tommy a small service. It was during one of my breaks in Glasgow from my time on the cruise liners. I was having a drink in Lauder's when in walked Tommy. We hadn't seen one another for a long time, for he had long since left Maryhill for the leafy and affluent suburb of Milngavie, taking his mother with him. We shot the breeze for a while about the old days, and he was interested to hear that I had become a croupier. He had never been in a casino, he said, he wasn't a gambling man, but he wouldn't mind having a visit to one just to see what went on. Did I think I could introduce him into one some night, just for the experience? So I phoned up the manager of the newly opened Stakis Princes casino in Sauchiehall Street, whom I knew well from my Chevalier days. My friend was not a member, I explained, nor was I, but did he think he could get us into the casino one night, as a favour to me for old time's sake? The next night we were standing in the games room of the Princes taking in the atmosphere, all of it brand new to Tommy who was standing there intoxicated by the novel experience. He was intoxicated in more ways than one, for he had been drinking a bit and was beginning to bet recklessly at the various tables, throwing money on as if it were confetti. I tried to bring some sort of pattern into his betting, and seeing that he was probably going to lose a lot of money if left to his own resources, each time he won a pot I creamed off some chips and put them safely away in my own pocket.

After an hour or so he began to tire of it all, searched his pockets for more money to lose and since he had none left decided to leave. He was in no condition to send home to his wife in Milngavie, so I took him home with me, where an obliging Rose put him up on the settee. Next morning, over the breakfast cup of tea I presented him with an envelope. In it were £2500 in notes, converted from the chips I had kept back the night before to save him from losing all the money he had with him. He couldn't thank me enough. I don't suppose £2500 meant much to him, but I couldn't have stood by and watched him throw it away and he appreciated that. I hadn't seen him since that time, but here he was now in the Casino Majorca. He was delighted to hear that I was here with Rose and the family. He had a yacht moored close by in the Puerto Portals marina. Did I think the family would like a wee cruise on it?

I was just at the end of my shift, so we went along to the bungalow, where Rose was delighted to see him again. After a bit of chit-chat the trip on the yacht was suggested. It wasn't just a run along the coast that Tommy had in mind. Why not a full-fledged Mediterranean trip up to Marseilles, then along the coast to Monte Carlo and back? The yacht was a big 60-footer with plenty of accommodation, he said. He and his wife Alice had been running it for the last couple of years as their hobby, and they had sailed it round the Med on several occasions. For this trip Tommy would bring along a professional sailor they sometimes hired for long journeys, he said. We went round to the marina and we were introduced to Alice his wife, a pleasant and charming girl from the West End of Glasgow, and Rose and the kids took to her right away. I don't know anything about yachts, but this one seemed like the absolute last word, with two tall masts and every conceivable electronic seafaring gadget, and with three small but luxurious cabins below decks. The kids jumped for joy at the prospect of a cruise on it, and the matter was settled. I asked for a few days leave, which was no problem since the casino was so quiet, and off we set for a marvellous few days cruising on the mirror-calm waters of the Mediterranean.

We had a fairly long sail across to Barcelona, done during the night as we slept and with the hired sailor in charge, then cruised along the coast to Marseilles, Toulon, Cannes, Nice and Monte Carlo. It was maybe a bit boring for the kids after the initial novelty of the trip had worn off, but for Rose and I it was absolutely wonderful. For me especially, for I was able at last to set foot in the casinos of Nice and Monte Carlo which I had so much wanted to do during my stint on the cruise ships. The only point of similarity between the Nice and Monte Carlo casinos and the Las Vegas ones is that gambling takes place in all these places. One can no more compare them than a Rolls Royce can be compared to a Ford.

Tommy stayed on in Majorca for a few more weeks and played some golf with us on Son Vida. Everybody there enjoyed his company. Great wealth had not changed him and as far as I was concerned he was still one of the Maryhill boys, somebody to drink a beer with and argue about the football.

FIFTEEN

HOME AGAIN

That year went by like a flash and the Majorcan contract drew to a close. Rose had enjoyed the year as much as I had. She had been back and forth from Glasgow several times and would not have refused the prospect of another spell in Majorca under the same circumstances, but when I tentatively approached the management for an extension of contract there was nothing forthcoming. The first year of the Casino Majorca had been anything but a great success, and from now on the house was going to be run along lines more suited to the package holiday trade. The services of rather expensive croupiers were no longer needed, so, somewhat reluctantly, for I had begun to enjoy the life of a Scots expatriate in Majorca, I packed everything up and returned to Glasgow. True for once to my promise to Rose, I put the thought of faraway casinos in exotic lands out of my mind. My years of working abroad and the short spell on the casino ships had been profitable, however. If I had stayed rooted to the one spot in Glasgow I would never have been able to provide for the family as well as I had done, and the little nest egg we now had in the bank would never have been laid. There is more to family life, however, than just providing the material things. I knew that I now should be providing the company and guidance to my children that certainly had been missing in my own formative years, and I realised too that I was missing the pleasure of seeing my three children develop into adults. I set my mind at rest; I would go back to the humdrum routine of a croupier in the Stakis organisation and lead the life of a normal family man.

Once back in Glasgow I was in no hurry to start work. When I was settled back into our three rooms and kitchen in Maryhill, all I wanted to do was wander around Glasgow, visit the old haunts and drink in the sights and sounds which I hadn't realised I had been missing so much. Many of the old familiar places I had hoped to visit had vanished in the surge of renewal and reconstruction that had started on the edges of the city centre. Albion Motors had gone and high-rise flats now stood where I had once matched coloured wire to colour wire. Garscube Road had all but vanished and I had to think hard before I could visualise where Vincent Coia's pie factory once stood. The tenements that once surrounded Partick Thistle's Firhill had all been demolished, and the football ground stood out like a sore thumb in the empty land surrounding it. I went one Saturday to see the Rangers play there. Some other firm had got the old VC pie concession. The new pies tasted even worse than the old VC ones had.

The paint factory where I had learned so much from my foreman friend John McCluskey was now a garage, and John himself, who had contributed so much to my formative years and had introduced me to the world of books, had passed away. The canal banks where I used to meet an opponent for a 'square go' were overgrown with weeds and in a state of disrepair, with the water in the canal thick with stagnant mud. The Ruchill golf course where I used to nick golf balls had been cleared to make way for a housing estate. The Garrioch boxing club had disbanded, and all of my closest pals had taken the road to Canada or Australia. A bus ride to Sauchiehall Street to visit Johnny McMillan's gym was also fruitless. The gym where the greats of Scottish boxing had once trained and the billiard hall beneath it had gone, and in their place stood a brand new department store. There was no alternative to the bus, the old familiar tramcars had disappeared from the streets.

The tenements in Willock Street where I was brought up had been demolished, and my father and mother's marriage, such as it had been, had broken up. Now that her family was grown up and away from home my mother no longer had to put up with the constant uncertainty of life with Ricey Read. My father had not matured and had not acquired sense with the passing of the years; if anything he had become even more unpredictable in his behaviour and was constantly in and out of trouble. About a year after I had left for the Bahamas he got in with a really bad crowd. They opened up a wee shop at the corner of Firhill Street and Garscube Road, called it Sunbeam Electrics and used it to sell stolen TVs and radios and electrical stuff like that. They got nicked right away, and my father spent a year in Saughton prison for reset. I remember going through to Edinburgh during one of my leaves to visit him in jail, and I felt heart sorry to see him behind bars. Enough was finally enough for my mother and she had left him, the separation finally ending in divorce. She had found a new husband, a fella called Joe Graham, a nice quiet dependable man who was the very antithesis of my father, and together they had set up home in a flat in Queen Margaret Crescent. Her new marriage seemed to have taken years off her shoulders. Instead of the rather careworn and perpetually harassed woman of my boyhood days she was now alert, smartly dressed and very happy in her altered circumstances. I reflected on how hard it must have been for her to raise the family. It was a shame for my father, I suppose. He wasn't really a bad man and never in his life had he raised a hand to anyone in the family. There was just an irresponsible side to his character that seemed to prevent him from being an ordinary hard-working family man like most men are. I never stopped being fond of him and always went to see him during my visits home. I was at his bedside when he died in Ruchill hospital at just 69 years of age. He had gone steadily downhill in health after his release from prison and the separation from our mother.

As soon I was back home one of the first things Rose and I talked about was buying a place of our own with more space for the kids. We thought of moving somewhere out to the suburbs, Bearsden or Milngavie maybe, since we could now afford to think about buying something there, but that would have meant uprooting the children from their schools and from their friends. The youngest, Lorraine, was still in Garrioch Street Primary and the two boys, Raymond and Craig, had gone on to North Kelvinside Secondary where they were doing well and bringing home glowing reports from their teachers. We had visions of them going on to higher education and to the doors of opportunity that a diploma or degree could open for them. Moreover, neither Rose nor I particularly wanted to leave the district. Ever since the slums around that area had been demolished, the rowdy element who used to pester the neighbourhood had disappeared into the new housing schemes and that part of Maryhill had become a nice respectable district to live in, so we set about looking for something suitable in the same school catchment area.

We struck it lucky right away. In a cul-de-sac in Maryhill we found a building for sale. It consisted of a large ground-floor workshop with a sizeable house above it, completely self-contained and separated from the nearby tenements. Although it would require a bit of money plus a great deal of time and effort to bring it up to standard, we immediately saw the potential of the place. The workshop we could let out for some trade or other, and the house, which had a separate entrance, would be perfect as a family home.

Our offer to buy was accepted and we set to work getting the place in order. About three months and a few thousand pounds of expense later we moved our furniture in and settled down to enjoy our new home. The ground-floor workshop, which had been let out as a joiner's, was bringing us in some very welcome cash each week as rent, and things were beginning to settle into place. After the years of living in hotel rooms it was great to go home to your own place and eat home-cooked meals instead of a quick pizza or a stodgy plate of something from a cafeteria. It was great to do odd jobs around the house, and since ours was big and newly fitted out there were plenty of those that needed doing. It was great to be able to go down to the pub for a pint and have a blether with the locals. It was great to have the kids around and talk sport and football and go to Ibrox with them to see the Rangers when they were playing at home. I think about that quite a bit now, and how things are really decided for you at a time when you have no say in the matter. My mother was Catholic and very devout in her religion. Ricey Read, my father, was Protestant, and although he didn't have much to do with our upbringing I suppose that it was because of him that we went to a Protestant school and supported the Rangers. If it had been the other way round, my father a Catholic and my mother a Protestant, no doubt I would have ended up supporting the Celtic. Anyhow, now that we were well settled in I decided it was time to pay my old employers at the Stakis group a visit and see about earning some money again.

Things had changed at the Stakis organisation with the passing of the years. The Chevalier was scheduled to be taken over by the Glasgow Corporation and demolished to make way for the new Cowcaddens redevelopment, which was to include a new concert hall and access roads to a new motorway. The staff were to be relocated to other Stakis hotels and casinos. These had now proliferated in number, and in Scotland alone half a dozen prestigious hotels had been taken over and casinos added to them. All this was explained to me by Mr Stavros, the stern unsmiling manager who had supervised me as a rookie croupier and who was still in charge of the gaming rooms. He seemed pleased enough to see me, taking time to examine the raft of references I had acquired during my travels, and asking me questions about the various casinos I had dealt in. The situation had changed a lot since I had first worked for him, he explained. He was now in overall charge of six casinos in Scotland, and this posed staff problems in the event of a croupier not turning up for duty at any of them. Some were fairly far removed from any centre that he could draw on for relief crews, and he was in the process of forming what he called a flying squad of a few skilled men, who could go at a moment's notice to wherever required. Salary and conditions were mentioned, and although the money fell far short of what I had become accustomed to in the past few years, the use of a car was included in the offer and having done my homework I knew that I could do no better anywhere in Scotland. A handshake settled the deal, and I was asked to present myself in a few days for the signing of contracts.

My base of operations was to be in my first place of work, the Regency in Waterloo Street, and there I took up my stance at the roulette table as if I had never been away from it. The décor of the place had changed; everything was a little bit more sumptuous and ornate than I remembered it, but the customers and the routine had not. First you had to change into your pocketless outfit in the locker room, the one place where the furnishings were just as basic as when I had left them, then submit to an inspection by the floor manager who had to satisfy himself that no aperture where chips could be hidden had been left in any part of your clothing. Hands and nails were also inspected for cleanliness, and a cursory glance sufficed to confirm that you had made use of a razor that morning, procedures which were common to all of the casinos I had worked in overseas.

The punters at the Regency conformed to the same stereotypes as before, however. In the afternoon the same overpainted, overdressed, overweight, overwealthy women wearing the same ostentatious jewellery sat themselves down at a table and made small bets of a size not commensurate with the aura of wealth they exuded. That was the first great difference to what I had been accustomed to in my travels abroad. In Vegas and in the Bahamas women dressed in simple slacks and blouse would carry satchels stuffed with dollars, and think nothing of making $1000 bets on the turn of a card or on the roll of the dice. On the cruise ships dress was equally casual, and in the Casino Majorca anything short of a bikini was in order, although the bets there could barely have bought you a Coca-Cola at the bar. Here in Waterloo Street women wearing thousands of pounds worth of clothes and jewellery made a big thing of placing a £20 bet on a card or on a number on a roulette wheel. Another thing that struck me at the Regency was that I never once saw a woman roll dice at the craps table. Maybe it was not ladylike for Bearsden and Newton Mearns ladies to do anything as common and as vulgar as shaking and rolling a set of dice in the way the broads did in Vegas.

The night-time punters had not changed much either. There was plenty of money on the tables, but the general atmosphere was much more sedate and tranquil than the frenetic buzz and noise of the Vegas scene. Perhaps the lack of one-armed bandits had something to do with it, for the Stakis casinos still frowned on the use of slot machines, which they reckoned lowered the tone of a place.

It wasn't as if Reo Stakis didn't realise the profit to be made from these machines, for a few yards round the corner from the Regency, in Hope Street, there was a spacious amusement arcade furnished with all the latest in mechanical and electronic gaming machines. The place was packed from early morning till late at night, with people of all ages and of all sexes frantically pumping money into them and pulling levers in the best tradition of their Las

Vegas counterparts. This strictly downmarket so-called amusement arcade formed a discreet and unpublicised part of the Stakis empire, but yard for yard it was probably just as profitable as the casinos. There were in Glasgow several other such amusement arcades, all in close proximity to a luxurious casino and all owned by the Stakis organisation.

These gaming machines had to be emptied of their money two or more times a day, and it was part of my job as a general factotum to carry out this function on occasion. Accompanied by two stalwart bodyguards I would do the rounds and empty the money boxes into leather money bags to be stacked in a strong-room at the back of each of the premises. Decimalisation had been introduced, the pound coin was now in circulation and was needed to operate the machines. I must have handled tens of thousands of these coins in the course of a day's work. Needless to say, the clothes I wore on these occasions were pocketless, as were those of my bodyguards.

Having to travel to outlying casinos was not without its adventurous side. Late one afternoon, no sooner had I changed into my casino clothes than a call came in. I was to go to Kilmacolm Hydro, where the croupier had taken suddenly ill while on duty, and a replacement was urgently needed. Get your car and off you go, said Stavros, so I jumped into my car dressed as I was, and about an hour or so later there I was, slightly breathless, spinning the roulette wheel in the Kilmacolm casino. I had a long shift to do, and was relieved for a fifteen minute break each two hours by the floor manager. The gaming rooms closed at about three in the morning, and bone-weary I set off in my car for the hour's drive back to Glasgow. About five miles out of Kilmacolm I became aware of a car fifty yards or so behind me, and suddenly there was the flash of a revolving blue light and a police car accelerated to a few feet in front of me and slowly forced me to a stop. The constable in the passenger seat got out, motioned my window down, stuck his head through and began sniffing audibly at me. I hadn't touched a drink for days, so I had no qualms about that. He looked at me for a few seconds, then informed me accusingly that one of my rear lights was not working.

By this time he had been joined by his mat,e who also had his head stuck through the passenger window. I told them I was sorry but both lights were working when I had left Glasgow. There was a pause. Could they see my driving licence please? Reflex action guided my hand to the hip pocket where I normally kept my wallet with my documents, and I froze when I encountered the stitched-up pocket. I tried to explain to the two sceptical policemen. They looked at me suspiciously and would have none of it, so I found myself following the police car back to the Kilmacolm police station, with one of the officers seated beside me. Two hours they kept me there, presumably checking up on my story about the sewn-up pockets, then finally let me go, with the stern injunction to have the defective light repaired and to present my driving licence at the nearest police station within the next three days.

I had some job convincing Rose that I hadn't invented the story as an excuse for my delay in getting home!

The Kilmacolm croupier had been hospitalised with a burst appendix, so my instructions were to report there every day until his return. Needless to say I gave my lights a careful inspection each night before setting out on the journey.

Compared to what I had been used to in Las Vegas and even in the Regency, Kilmacolm Hydro was a fairly tame affair. There were two roulette tables, four card tables and a crap game. Weekday business was light, with customers consisting mainly of local punters coming in at night for a flutter, with no great amount of money passing over the tables. At weekends there was a fair amount of activity, enough to keep boredom at bay, with the occasional high flier stirring things up with bets in the thousands. Tame and sedate the casino certainly was, but it was in that tranquil environment that I was given the biggest fright I have ever experienced in my working life in the casinos.

I was working as croupier at one of the roulette tables one week-night, with only three or four players making some unexciting bets, and with the inspector almost dozing with boredom on his high chair. A tall, quietly dressed youngish man of about 35 or so, carrying a small attaché case, positioned himself at the table, deposited the case at his feet and brought out some money from it. He handed me over twenty-five £20 notes, which I changed into chips. He waited for one or two spins of the wheel to be made before betting and then placed the £500 worth of chips on number 19. I waited for all bets to be made, called out the usual announcement that bets were now closed, and spun the wheel.

Number 19 did not come up. Impassively, the young man counted out another five hundred pounds, which I again changed into chips, which again were placed on the same number. Again another number came up. A hundred times that same procedure was repeated without a single word being uttered by the player. Five hundred pounds worth of chips bought, bet and lost, always on number 19. Over the space of four hours or so the man had lost £50,000 on that same number. His face did not change expression. The attaché case now lay empty on the floor. He put his hands in his pockets, pulled out the empty linings and spoke his first words of the night.

'I've no fucking money left, but I've got this,' he shouted, his face suddenly contorted with rage, and pulled out a revolver from his belt. He stuck it over the table and aimed it at my face.

'Spin that fucking wheel again, and if 19 comes up, you're a dead man.'

The pit boss was standing at the table, speechless. Again came the strangled yell: 'Spin that fucking wheel!' and the gun was pointed straight at me. Out of the corner of my eye I could see two bouncers standing by, attracted to the table by the shouts, but not daring to make a move in case the gun should go off. The pit boss came up close to me and whispered: 'Spin it, but if 19 comes up, call another number.'

Hypnotised by the waving gun, I looked straight at the man and spun the wheel as if in a dream. His staring eyes were fixed on my face, paying no attention to the spinning wheel. As the wheel stopped and the ball clattered into a number my eyes were still frozen on the gun. I heard the pit boss shout out: 'Twenty-two'. Without shifting his gaze from me the young man lowered the revolver and went to put it back in his belt. He had not looked down to check the number for himself. Before he could do so about 35 stones of bone and muscle in the form of the two bouncers wrestled him to the floor. The police were called and the man taken away. The gun was fully loaded. The pit boss had called correctly. The ball had come to rest on number 22.

I've been in some sleazy dives in my time. I've dealt cards to gamblers who looked as if they could cut your heart out if you dealt them a losing card. I've seen a knife pulled at a crap table over a set of loaded dice in Vegas, and a player stabbed. I've seen police break up riots in gambling dens in Glitter Gulch. I've seen six-guns brandished, but never once did I ever feel personally threatened. Until one calm and tranquil night in the most unlikely of places, Kilmacolm Hydro. I wasn't worth a button for the rest of the night!

After that incident, nothing of any note happened to break the daily routine of dealing and spinning and stacking. I was moved around from casino to casino as the need arose, sometimes a spell at Dunblane Hydro, sometimes one at the Regency and once, for a short time, to a new casino just opened by the Stakis organisation in Manchester. These travels gave rise to one or two adventures.

One day I was told to report to Dunblane Hydro together with another croupier, an Italian by the name of Marco. He had his own car, a snazzy MG sports drophead coupé, and since it was a beautiful day we decided to travel up with it. The car bore the registration number '8 EXY', but Marco, being a bit of a nut really, had blanked out one of the upstrokes on the 8, making the number read as 'SEXY'. A few miles out of Glasgow, travelling at about 60 miles an hour or so, even though the speed limit on that stretch of road was 40, we were forced to slow down behind a long queue of cars stretching ahead for about 500 yards. The speedometer needle fell to just under 40 miles per hour. Minutes passed and Marco became impatient at what he considered to be a slow crawl. He swung out, dropped a gear for maximum acceleration, pressed down hard on the pedal and proceeded to overtake the long line of cars. The MG was now doing about 80 miles per hour. He raced past the car at the head of the queue, pulled in and saw to his horror that the car was in fact a police vehicle. There was a wailing of siren, a flashing of lights, and the ashen-faced Marco slowed down sharply and pulled over to the side of the road. He faced a battery of charges, including that of falsifying a number plate and dangerous driving. The police were decent enough to let us drive into Dunblane behind them, but subsequently Marco had to appear in court, where he was given a stiff fine and banned from driving for a year.

I once did the Glasgow–Dunblane journey tucked up awkwardly in the boot of an E-Type Jaguar. Yet again after an emergency call, three of us were told to report to the Hydro. There were two cars available, my own, which was a four-seater saloon, and one other, a two seater E-Type Jaguar. My car refused to start. There was no option, we had to go in the Jaguar, and in that car there was only room for two. I was the smallest of the three, so into the boot I went. It took days for the aches to disappear from my bones!

SIXTEEN

FOUR HILLS

For a few months now I had become aware that my fingers were not as nimble or as accurate in handling cards and chips as they once had been. Slight things and barely noticeable to an onlooker, but very worrying to me. Where before I could unerringly count a pile of chips with a quick riffle of the fingers and without looking, now at times I had to riffle twice and help myself with a quick glance downwards. Once or twice a chip would slip from my fingers and roll along the table, to be stopped and returned by my stacker. Such things can happen to all croupiers, but they had never happened to me. After all, I kept telling myself, I'm as good as any in the business and these things just don't happen to the best. I felt that I had become slower in dealing from the card shoe, and there were times I could feel myself making a clumsy shuffle of the cards. Although the pit bosses had as yet not noticed, I had begun to make the odd clumsy throw at the craps table. I didn't seem able to get the proper feel of the dice in my fingers. In the morning I would sometimes waken with my hands hot and tingling, with the signet ring I wore feeling too tight on my middle finger.

'You've got the beginning of arthritis in your hands,' pronounced the family doctor. 'No pain? OK, then, it might never come to anything, and even if it does you can live to 90 with it. Come back and see me in six months.' And he sent me off with some aspirin.

Very, very gradually, the change in my accuracy and speed of dealing increased to the point where it was noted by the pit bosses, and I found myself in his office being spoken to by a sympathetic Mr Stavros. I must realise that he couldn't leave me on the floor as a dealer, he said, when I explained my condition to him. But there was always room for an inspector or a pit boss in the gaming rooms, and he wouldn't like to lose a person with my experience. Think about it, he said. Take a couple of weeks holiday and come back and we'll talk about it. There was really not much to think about. It was obvious to me that

I couldn't continue for very long dealing at the tables. My hands weren't getting any worse, but they weren't getting any better either, and the fact that I was so focused on my fingers seemed to multiply my clumsiness with the cards and chips. I needed to work at something, so I told Mr. Stavros that I was ready to take on the job of inspector.

Right from the very beginning I did not like my new duties one little bit. I felt like a parole officer in charge of a room full of jailbirds let out of prison on trust. I realised of course that when employees are dealing with tens and hundreds of thousands in cash, some of them must be tempted to cream off a little for themselves if they can find a way, and that a strict code of behaviour must be applied to eliminate the possibility of dishonesty amongst them. As a dealer I was quite happy to abide by the rules. I had to make sure that all my pockets were sewn up, I had to shuffle and deal cards in a specific manner so that the possibility of cheating was reduced to a minimum, I had to show the palms of my hands whenever I wanted to leave the gaming table for whatever reason. All that I was quite happy to do. That was my responsibility and I accepted those constraints as part of my job. As a dealer I had to make sure that the players at my particular table were playing by the rules and not attempting to cheat the house in any way, and that was perfectly acceptable too. My gaming table was my domain and I ran it by the rules of the house and I myself behaved according to those same rules.

To make sure that everyone else is abiding by these rules is another matter. My experience was that 99.99% of dealers are honest under all circumstances, but as an inspector you have to be suspicious of everybody. As far as you, an inspector, are concerned, there are no honest men in your part of the gaming room. All must be considered as potential thieves, employees as well as the players. I did not mind supervising the actions of the players. They come to the casino to win and you expect them to use any means to do so if they can get away with it. But as an inspector no one has to be taken on trust, not even your own colleagues; everyone has to be regarded as potentially dishonest. As an inspector you have to sit at the top of a roulette table and watch every single move that takes place. You have to watch the bets being placed to ensure they are placed properly and you must pay particular attention to see that the correct winnings are paid over for late bets at the roulette table. That is the croupier's job, of course, but you have to double-check for the possibility of collusion, or deal with a complaint from a punter about the odds on a particular win. If there is heavy play at a card table you have to stand by and observe the play closely. If a dealer wants to go to the toilet he has to show you the palms of his hands, which at first always made me want to laugh; it reminded me of myself at school raising my hand to the teacher with the words, 'Please miss, may I leave the room?'

As a dealer you always have friends amongst the other dealers and croupiers and sometimes go out for a drink or a game of golf together. As an inspector you feel yourself just that wee bit different, and nobody seeks out your company in off-duty moments. I remembered what my old foreman John McCluskey used to say about policemen. They develop a mentality of their own, he used to tell me. They never really make any friends amongst their neighbours, because they never know when they might have to arrest one of them for something or other. Then of course you yourself are under the scrutiny of the pit boss, who has no fixed stance on the floor, but wanders at will overseeing everything. If a particular table under your supervision as an inspector encounters a prolonged losing streak you must alert the pit boss and he may decide to change over that dealer, which made me feel as if I personally were apportioning blame for a streak of bad luck.

The Stakis casinos were known to be very strict in their teaching methods and in their demands for disciplined behaviour on the part of their dealers, and indeed, this was one of the reasons why Stakis-trained dealers and croupiers were one of the principal targets for personnel poachers from other casinos. As a dealer, I personally had no problem in adhering to any rule laid down; I just did not like having to enforce them. Stakis himself was a very pleasant and fair employer, but on the casino floor he had a superstitious side to his character, which at times I found irksome as an inspector. He visited the casinos regularly and inspected everything closely. He hated to see anything even slightly out of place, and would blame a losing streak at a table on the fact that a picture was not properly aligned on an adjacent wall, or on the fact that the dealer's bow tie was slightly askew, or that an ashtray on a nearby table had not been emptied, or that a flower arrangement was not properly placed, deficiencies which he would instruct the pit boss or the inspector to remedy so that the bad luck would change. No, I did not enjoy the job of inspector at all, but it was a job and it brought in a regular salary, and I suppose that really was all that should have mattered.

I began to find that spare time was hanging heavily on my hands. I had all but given up golf. In the States and in Majorca I had played for the sake of the companionship and for the enjoyment of the fine weather on the courses there, but I was not keen enough to play golf in the Scottish wind and rain. I had long since finished all the odd jobs I had to do around the house, so to help fill in my free time I took to helping out in the workshop on the ground floor. I had always liked to mess about with tools, but as a dealer my hands always had to be immaculately manicured, so I couldn't afford to get any cuts or bruises, or dirt under my fingernails. As an inspector, however, that didn't matter so much, so I could potter about to my heart's content and not worry if I split a fingernail or if I had to come into the gaming room with a piece of sticking plaster on a knuckle. Sometimes too at weekends I would help out at the Punch Bowl bar at Maryhill Cross. It was a busy pub and packed to the doors on a Friday and Saturday, and there one night I met an old pal from my boxing days at the Garrioch Club.

I hadn't seen John McNulty for years. When I was boxing in the Scottish amateur team as a flyweight he was in the light heavyweight division, so we never fought one another but used to train and spar together a lot at Johnny McMillan's gym in Sauchiehall Street. He was now in business on his own, he told me. He ran a small security company which specialised in guarding building sites, of which there were many now in the Glasgow area. These sites were full of valuable material. Lead, copper, bathroom and kitchen fittings were scattered all over them for the taking and were an attraction for thieves, so precautions had to be taken, day and night, to ensure that pilfering was kept to a minimum. He asked me round to his office, where I was quite impressed with the organisation he had built up. He was having problems with staff, he told me. The foreman in charge of a big site was going to be off ill for quite some time, and he was going to be hard put to get a temporary replacement. He looked at me hopefully. Did I work every weekend at the Punch Bowl? Just occasionally? That was great. How would I like to supervise that site for a couple of nights at weekends for him until the foreman came back? I laughed at first. What did I know about security and how to look after the sort of places he ran security for? Nothing to it, he said. All you do is sit in an office and watch a couple of TV monitors. You'll have two men to do the donkey work. They'll patrol the area and report back to you every so often, and if there's any trouble you just give the police a buzz and they'll sort things out for you. Come on, Archie, just for two nights a week until Alf the foreman gets back, and there's a good few quid in cash in it for you. The hourly rate was more or less what I would have been getting at the Punch Bowl, and the mention of cash was a big incentive.

I decided to give it a try. The two nights concerned were Friday and Saturday, which meant that I had all day Sunday to catch up on sleep. I had to convince Rose that I was actually staying away from home to act as a glorified night watchman, as she called it, and not playing fast and loose with somebody else, but she finally said OK with a shake of the head, as if to signify that something was not quite right with mine. The site that John McNulty had to keep secure was one of about ten acres or so just off Bilsland Drive, opposite the old Ruchill hospital. The area, not a very salubrious one, was in the process of redevelopment, and surrounded by derelict tenements due for demolition but still partially occupied. There was a high incidence of unemployment in the district, an air of neglect and decay lay over everything, and the valuable and easily stolen material on the building site would have acted like a magnet for the local hooligans. The site was being developed by a company, the Westminster Health Care Group, and the building was designated to be a purpose-built nursing home for leasing to the Greater Glasgow Health Board when completed in eighteen months time or so.

John McNulty had been right; the two beat men, as he called them, did their job well, they patrolled the grounds at intervals and made sure that the battery of CCTV cameras erected on the high wire fence surrounding the site were in proper working order, and I had nothing to do apart from sitting in front of TV monitors and making sure that regular inspections were made of the grounds. Never once in the four weeks that I was on duty there did I have occasion to get in touch with the police; the security system put in place by John was much too tight for any petty thieves to get the better of. Nor did I lose much sleep. There was so little for me to do that I spent most of the time dozing in front of the monitors, and did not feel in the slightest deprived of sleep the next morning. Alf the foreman came back to his work after a month, John McNulty thanked me for helping him out and I went back to sleeping in my own bed on Fridays and Saturdays.

However, the germ of an idea had taken root as I sat in the little heated hut on the Westminster building site. I was fed up with the work at the casinos, and did not relish the thought of finishing the rest of my working life perched on a stool over a roulette table, bored out of my skin and inhaling second-hand tobacco smoke. Truth to tell, I was fed up to the teeth. Sitting there night after night just watching others deal and spin the wheel was becoming a penance. As a croupier and dealer I had enjoyed the action and mental stimulation involved in spinning the roulette wheel, in dealing the cards, in taking the bets and paying out the winnings, but I was beginning to hate the passive role I now had on the casino floor.

I could afford to take a gamble on something else. The family was up and educated now. Raymond had a first-class position as a computer graphics designer, Craig had a place as a clerk in the Procurator Fiscal's office, and Lorraine could look forward to a career as an Inland Revenue inspector. There was just Rose and myself to think about now. I had discovered that once the building was finished and handed over to the Westminster Trust, they themselves, in some form of partnership with the Greater Glasgow Health Board, would be providing the nursing staff for the home, and that security for the nursing home would be given out to some independent security company or other. I approached John McNulty. Would he have any interest in providing security for the nursing home once it was built? No, he said, once it was finished he would move on to some other site and the owners would make their own arrangements about security. What was involved in setting up a security company, I wondered. What qualifications were needed to get a licence or whatever it was you needed to operate? He explained. First of course you had to be given a clean bill of health from the police. Then you had to sit exams to get certificates from the fire authorities, the City & Guild and the British Security Industry Association to show that you were qualified in fire-fighting techniques, in first aid and in advanced security procedures, and then you could set up your own company if you wanted to.

I told him what I had in mind. I was toying with the idea of setting myself up in business and offering my services to the Westminster Trust as someone who would take over the security arrangements at their new nursing home. That would give me about a year to study up on regulations and get whatever certificates were necessary, and since he was a good pal and had no interest in the job himself he would, I was sure, give me all the hints I needed about operating procedures. John was more than helpful. Since I would be not be competing with him he was only too pleased to show me the way to go about getting all the qualifications I would need. I studied hard at classes for a few hours each week, and after about six months I was the proud possessor of all the necessary certificates. I also put in some practical work on some of John's sites, and drew up a prospectus for presentation to the Westminster management when the time should arrive.

I had said not a word of all this to Rose, and there was a major explosion when I did. What was the matter with my present job, she asked. I was earning good money, why throw it all away for an uncertain future? I would be no better off as far as money was concerned. I might even be worse off, and what would happen if the Westminster people were not happy with me and showed me the door? All perfectly valid comments, but I had made up my mind, I said. Even if this opportunity had not presented itself I could not have carried on as a casino inspector. I would have looked for something, anything, just to get away from an ambience that was rapidly becoming suffocating to me. So Rose threw up her hands, said I had gone crazy, but if that was what I wanted, again so be it.

The Westminster site was rapidly approaching completion and the moment for decisions had arrived. I took a deep breath and submitted my application to take over the security for Four Hills Nursing Home. The Glasgow Health Board was not yet involved at this stage, and the building was still being managed by Mr Tom Docherty of the Westminster Group, who had to decide the allocation of the security contract. With no experience behind me I considered the little company I had set up to be the least favoured of the applicants, but my recently acquired qualifications were so impressive, my prospectus had been so well prepared and I came across so well on interview that, much to my delight and surprise, I was awarded the contract. I promptly handed in my notice at the casino, and three weeks later I sat down proudly at my new place of work, the reception desk of Four Hills.

Fronted by a spacious landscaped car park, Four Hills nursing home was set in an oasis of green landscaped gardens, in stark contrast to the surrounding waste ground and dingy tenements. It was not yet operational, but was in the final stages of being fitted out and staffed. The accommodation consisted of a ground floor and an upper floor, each floor having a wing on either side of the main entrance. The reception area had its own little lounge and could well have been that of a small hotel. On one side there was the manager's office, now occupied by the briskly efficient Heather McPhee, and on the other the reception desk. Behind this desk was a room for the office staff, and on the other side a corridor led on to the gleaming stainless steel equipped kitchens. The wings, or wards as they really were, bore the names of four of the local districts, Maryhill, Ruchill, Firhill and Lambhill, hence the overall name of Four Hills. Each wing had 30 individual bedrooms furnished to a high standard, all with TV and en suite bathrooms. Each wing had its own dining room plus two large drawing rooms, all with large bay windows and furnished and decorated to a standard worthy of a four-star hotel. Two spacious lifts, each capable of accommodating two wheelchairs, serviced the first floor, which could also be accessed by a stairway. At the top of the stairs a hall led to a hairdressing boutique and a small private sitting room for the use of visitors. All bedrooms and public areas were fully carpeted, with curtains to match.

The facilities in the home were of the highest order. They were equipped with shower rooms and bathrooms specially designed for the elderly and incapacitated, together with rooms for physiotherapy and for the changing of dressings. The latest in hoists and trolleys for the management of completely immobilised patients were available. Each patient was to have his or her own wheel chair, with motorised models available for special cases. These were marvels of medical design, which the completely paralysed patient could manoeuvre simply by movements of the lips or mouth.

It was my duty and that of the three men I employed to keep the buildings and grounds secure and under observation at all times. To this end, each of the buildings was fitted with a number of closed-circuit TV cameras, with a bank of monitors situated behind the reception desk. These cameras scanned all paths and open areas. The entire complex was surrounded by a wall and chain-linked fence and could be accessed only through a double metal gate, electrically controlled from the reception desk. My security duties had also an internal aspect. Some of the patients were ambulatory, so care had to be taken that they did not stray outside into danger, and alarmed fire exits had to be monitored.

As the wards filled up with patients the home began to acquire a general air of purpose and caring. The rooms were occupied by the frail and the very ill, all of them elderly and all in need of 24 hour personal care. Most were incapable of movement and had to have every bodily need attended to, others so incapacitated that supervision was always necessary lest they do themselves harm. The nurses and auxiliary staff went about their business with care and humanity. Our old family doctor used to say that the best medicine was TLC, tender loving care, and in the wards of Four Hills that medicine was liberally dispensed.

My work could not have been further removed from my casino activities. I cannot deny that I initially derived satisfaction from my work in the casinos. I took pride in my skill and ability as a croupier and as a dealer, but that was mixed in with a dislike and contempt for the people I came into contact with. There everything was geared to the satisfaction of greed and the pursuit of pleasure. Here all was geared to the alleviation of suffering and the care of those about to depart from this life. In all of the jobs I had ever had, the VC pies, the paint factory, Albion Motors, the King's Theatre, the various casinos I had worked in, I had never been really content, I had never really felt satisfied with what I was doing. In my early jobs all I was concerned with was the pay packet at the end of the week. In the casinos money seemed to have no value other than that of feeding the greed of the gamblers, and I had grown tired of the sight of rapacious faces with avid eyes fixed on the spin of a wheel or the turn of a card or the fall of the dice. But in Four Hills I was content with what I was now doing. I felt that in coming here I was being paid at last for doing something of value in life; I was contributing to the care and well-being of the old and the very sick who had come to this place to end their lives in peace and dignity.

At the beginning of my career at Four Hills ten years ago I received two letters, one from the incoming manager, Heather McPhee, and one from the relatives of a terminally ill patient. They lit a warm glow within me, never

experienced before, which persists to the present day. The one from Heather
read:

> Dear Archie,
> Many thanks for the beautiful flowers. I appreciate your kindness. It
> certainly took away the apprehension of coming to Four Hills. With some-
> one like you supporting me I should do fine.
> Love,
> Heather

And the other:

> Dear Archie,
> Happy Birthday and good wishes for this and all the others that follow.
> It must be so difficult always to be so nice and cheery to so many awkward
> people, myself included. You make it look all so simple and effortless. Thank
> you for all your kindnesses on our behalf.
> Ann and Isa

Last year Rose and I went on a package holiday tour of California and the western states of the USA. The trip, which took in San Francisco and the Grand
Canyon, included a three-day stay in Las Vegas at one of the new hotel-casino
complexes, the Luxor, an opulent 2000-room monster Egyptian theme-park that
could have swallowed up without trace half a dozen of the places I worked in
during my days in Vegas. The city has almost tripled in size since I knew it, and
the Strip now boasts of a dozen or so of these massive complexes, among them
the Venetian, the Hilton Grand, the MGM Grand, Treasure Island and the
Tuscany, none of which would not be out of place in Disneyland. Bugsy
Seigel's Flamingo, now part of the Hilton chain, was rebuilt six years ago and
is now one of the biggest hotels in the world, with a staggering 3000 rooms.
Benny Binion is long gone, but his Horseshoe is there and is still owned by
the Binion family. It is bigger and brighter and more ostentatious than it was 30
years ago when I dealt poker there, but somehow, despite the six-guns and Win-
chester rifles displayed on the walls, it has lost the realistic cowboy atmosphere
of the original. The Desert Inn is closed and derelict, to be rebuilt I was told, but
the golf course behind was still there, unchanged from the days I used to play a
$20 Nassau with Amarillo Slim and his companions. I went in search of the
Gamblers' Bookshop and found it, almost lost in a sea of buildings where before
there had been open land. Jack and Jean Luckman have long passed on, but their
sons still run the business. The interior has been modernised, and carries a huge
stock of books and videos on every aspect of gambling, but 'Eulogy to a Gambler' still hangs on the wall. There was, of course, no sign of any familiar face
from my days in Vegas 30-odd years ago. In my day, Luckman's Gamblers' Bookshop was the only one in Vegas. I now counted 27 in the phone book.

We have been to Majorca many times on holiday during the last 15 years and have tried to make our holidays coincide with the annual 9.30 Society's Ladies' Night dinner, so as to meet old friends and golfing companions, or what is left of them. Although the Society still exists, it is now down to a handful of ageing members who are allowed the use of the old starting time only through the good offices of the old Spanish starter Eustacio, who has been with the club since the beginning. He squeezes them in between the groups of package tour golfers who now crowd the golf course, a practice which would be frowned upon by the new German owners of the Son Vida Hotel and golf course. The new owners have no time for a tradition which takes over valuable time on the first tee, and they look upon the course as simply an asset which has to be exploited to the full. In a very short while the 9.30 Golfing Society of Son Vida will cease to exist. The Casino Majorca is still there, packed to the doors with holidaymakers who come to gamble with a few hundred euros. To me it now seems more like a glorified amusement arcade than a casino.

I have taken a great deal of pleasure in showing Rose all the places I knew and worked in so many years ago, and we plan to visit the Bahamas some day. Perhaps when I start drawing the old-age pension in a couple of years time.

The Wheel of Fortune spins for all of us, and sooner or later it will stop for all of us. When the wheel comes to rest, who knows what lies in store?

EPILOGUE
by
JOE PIERI

On the 14th of September 2003 my wife Mary passed away. Eighteen months had gone by since she was admitted to Four Hills. During this time her condition had deteriorated to the point that she could no longer make any co-ordinated movement and could do nothing for herself. For a year and a half she had been well looked after and her nurses and carers could not have been more dedicated. She was fed and washed and changed several times each day, and lay on an airbed to prevent the formation of bedsores. She had been made as comfortable as was humanly possible. I visited her twice each day, morning and afternoon. She could not communicate in any way, her facial expression never changed and it was impossible to say to what extent she was aware of her condition and of her surroundings, if at all. She slept most of the time, but in her waking moments her eyes followed my movements around the room, and I like to think that she was aware of my presence and that my being there beside her brought her some comfort.

It is a terrible thing to watch a person you have loved and lived with for more than 50 years disintegrate and decline in such a fashion, but the pain of seeing her so had dulled over these months and I had been able to come to terms with the sadness of her condition and the certainty of the final end. In this I was helped by the sympathy and understanding of old friends, and of the many new friends I made amongst those who minister to her needs.

Most of us will at some point will grow old, take ill and will be in need of care and attention. When the inevitable comes knocking at my door I could hope for no better place to be admitted than to Four Hills Nursing Home and to be placed under the dedicated care of the management there.

Perhaps the one thing above all else that helped me come to terms with the fate that had befallen Mary was the friendship I made with a long-term resident of Four Hills, May Chesser, who during her active years was the secretary of a school in Cumbernauld. May was widowed some 30 years ago and has one son, an electrical engineer who works and lives permanently in the

Dominican Republic. She is a woman of 74 years of age whose smooth, unwrinkled face belies her years. For twenty years she has suffered from multiple sclerosis and for more than 10 of those years she has been left completely paralysed from the neck downwards, unable literally to move a finger. Everything has to be done for her. She has to be fed, washed and dressed and hoisted into a specially constructed electrically powered reclining wheelchair which she controls by the movement of her mouth on a projecting lever.

May's mind is completely unaffected by her illness. Mentally alert, she makes full use of her every waking moment. She listens to the news on the radio and keeps abreast of world events. She listens to music, watches chosen programmes and videos on TV and is particularly fond of romantic musicals. Her current favourite is an old film of forty or more years ago, *Three Coins in the Fountain*, which she asks to be shown time and time again. She does not like to watch sad films, for she cannot wipe her own tears from her eyes and has to wait for a passing carer to perform that simple task for her. She takes a keen interest in the happenings at Four Hills and is always concerned about the well-being of the staff and of other residents. She has never been heard to utter a single word of complaint.

I can think of no greater tragedy than to be a thinking, living, reasoning personality, with a brain imprisoned for evermore in a wasted unresponsive body, and yet May is tranquil and happy in the acceptance of her fate. She is a joy to be with and to talk to, and radiates an inner serenity which reflects the depth of her religious belief. I stop at her room every morning for a chat, and never cease to marvel at the happiness and peace of mind with which she greets the arrival of a new day. My contact with her has enriched my own life, for she is a shining example of how a person can come to terms with adversity. May has been an inspiration to me and to all who come into contact with her.

During the writing of this book I have come to understand fully why Archie Morrison draws such great personal satisfaction from the work he does at Four Hills, as opposed to what many would consider to be his glamorous and eventful life as the spinner of a roulette wheel and the dealer of gaming cards. It stems from the knowledge that with the others of the staff there he is making an essential contribution to the well-being of May Chesser and to the other 119 residents who are in need of care and personal attention.

In Archie I have discovered a kindred spirit whose formative background I myself have known well, and whose story I have taken great pleasure in telling.

Joe Pieri
Lenzie, 2004